NEW DIRECTIONS FOR INSTITUTIONAL RESEARCH

Patrick T. Terenzini
The Pennsylvania State University
EDITOR-IN-CHIEF

Ellen Earle Chaffee
North Dakota Board of Higher Education
ASSOCIATE EDITOR

Adapting Strategic Planning to Campus Realities

Frank A. Schmidtlein
University of Maryland

Toby H. Milton
Essex Community College

EDITORS

Number 67, Fall 1990

JOSSEY-BASS INC., PUBLISHERS
San Francisco

ADAPTING STRATEGIC PLANNING TO CAMPUS REALITIES
Frank A. Schmidtlein, Toby H. Milton (eds.)
New Directions for Institutional Research, no. 67
Volume XVII, Number 3
Patrick T. Terenzini, Editor-in-Chief
Ellen Earle Chaffee, Associate Editor

LC 85-645339   ISSN 0271-0579   ISBN 1-55542-809-6

NEW DIRECTIONS FOR INSTITUTIONAL RESEARCH is part of The Jossey-Bass Higher Education Series and is published quarterly by Jossey-Bass Inc., Publishers (publication number USPS 098-830). Second-class postage paid at San Francisco, California, and at additional mailing offices. Postmaster: Send address changes to Jossey-Bass Inc., Publishers, 350 Sansome Street, San Francisco, California 94104.

EDITORIAL CORRESPONDENCE should be sent to the Editor-in-Chief, Patrick T. Terenzini, Center for the Study of Higher Education, 133 Willard Building, The Pennsylvania State University, University Park, Pennsylvania 16802.

Photograph of the library by Michael Graves at San Juan Capistrano by Chad Slattery © 1984. All rights reserved.

Printed on acid-free paper in the United States of America.

CONTENTS

EDITORS' NOTES

Most planning literature describes how planning should be conducted. Although there have been many calls for colleges and universities to institute strategic planning, few describe how planning was actually performed. This volume seeks to remedy this lack of information on planning practices. Its principal purpose is to illustrate the diverse approaches colleges and universities might use to anticipate and adapt to changing opportunities and threats. In five case studies, college and university administrators describe how their institutions became aware of, and then tried to deal with, emerging issues and changing conditions. When considered together, these case studies highlight the creativity, sensitivity, and flexibility colleges and universities employ to respond to key institutional issues. They also provide new perspectives on how planning can be accomplished in higher education institutions.

During the past several decades, the use of formal planning in higher education has been widely advocated as necessary to ensure institutional survival and vitality. This advice is often interpreted to mean that one should apply one of the numerous planning processes described in the growing body of literature on higher education planning and management. Many campuses have tried to use comprehensive planning approaches that follow guidelines outlined in books or journals, recommended by planning consultants, or presented at workshops and seminars. Frequently, this practice has resulted in considerable frustration and disappointment as committees fail to reach consensus, faculty and departments steadfastly refuse to address critical issues, and expectations raised by the planning process far exceed available resources.

Despite the many obstacles to planning in higher education, there is considerable evidence that successful institutions do not ignore significant environmental changes or pressing internal problems. Instead of uncritically adopting a particular planning approach, they often engage in a broad range of activities—both in their attempts to address the potential impact of changing conditions on their mission and operations and in developing strategies to address these impacts. While some of these planning activities may incorporate recommended guidelines and models, others are uniquely designed to fit institutional cultures, decision processes, structures, and practices. Successful institutions appear to base their approach on the essential character of the issues they confront. Not infrequently, these approaches reflect alternative assumptions about how colleges and universities can perform the planning function.

Each of the five case studies in this volume examines how issues were defined and communicated and describes how strategies for addressing

NEW DIRECTIONS FOR INSTITUTIONAL RESEARCH, no. 67, Fall 1990 © Jossey-Bass Inc., Publishers

these issues were developed and implemented. The five institutions were selected because of their reported success in developing effective approaches for identifying and dealing with emerging threats and challenges. While each institution represents a different sector of higher education, many of the challenges they faced (and their responses to them) were not confined to any particular type of institution. Thus, their experiences may be useful to others facing similar circumstances at diverse institutions.

In Chapter One, Michael J. Dooris and G. Gregory Lozier point out how continuous attention to the design of formal planning helped overcome some common problems and facilitated dealing with changing concerns at The Pennsylvania State University. They emphasize the evolving nature of formal planning at their institution.

John A. Dunn, Jr., in Chapter Two, describes how presidential leadership was instrumental in promoting major institutional changes at Tufts University. His discussion of entrepreneurial planning shows how a president with vision and a willingness to take risks can gain the support needed to alter the character and direction of a private university.

The Bradford College story, told by Janice S. Green in Chapter Three, is perhaps the most dramatic example of change and revitalization in this volume. Again, presidential vision, effectively combined with prompt administrative attention to fundamental institutional functions, served as energizing forces for major change.

In Chapter Four, Peter A. M. Maassen and Michiel T. E. van Buchem discuss the story of the University of Twente in the Netherlands, another institution that underwent significant change. Their analysis shows how three key leaders helped shape new directions by carefully adapting formal planning concepts to alter the character of the university.

Philip M. Ringle and Frederick W. Capshaw, in Chapter Five, explain how Essex Community College, a basically healthy institution with a clearly defined mission, adapted to changing demands and circumstances. Their discussion illustrates how adopting planning processes to address particular issues can foster responsiveness and institutional change.

The concluding chapter analyzes the diverse campus approaches and points out the general features that characterized the various efforts. Findings from a recently completed nationwide study of campus planning activities are used to support this analysis. The chapter closes with some generalizations about the basic character of successful planning processes.

Frank A. Schmidtlein
Toby H. Milton
Editors

Frank A. Schmidtlein is associate professor of higher education in the Department of Education Policy, Planning, and Administration at the University of Maryland, College Park. He served as director of a nationwide study of institutional planning conducted by the National Center for Postsecondary Governance and Finance and is an associate director of the center.

Toby H. Milton is director of the Office of Institutional Studies and Analysis at Essex Community College in Baltimore County, Maryland. She served as associate director of the national center's institutional planning project and as the center's assistant director of operations.

Successful planning can draw from a variety of formal models. The experience of a large public university reveals important principles that can apply to many approaches.

Adapting Formal Planning Approaches: The Pennsylvania State University

Michael J. Dooris, G. Gregory Lozier

This chapter describes how over the past two decades one large public research university has used formal planning—both to absorb environmental shocks and solve pressing problems and to set new goals and undertake new initiatives. The lessons drawn from the case study are simple:

- Strategic planning, carefully conceived and carried out over time, can succeed in colleges and universities.
- No single model is right for all situations.
- An institution's planning process can, and probably should, be modified periodically to meet changing circumstances.
- Some general principles apply to each approach.

Sportswriter Red Smith began a book on fishing by warning, "Readers are advised to pursue this no further. Everything there is to say has been said already." This chapter might begin with a similar warning; it essentially expands upon and illustrates the four points listed above.

How is a college or university managed? Like any other organization— by people making and implementing decisions. But real-world managerial problems are seldom a matter of logical analysis or calculated choice among well-defined alternatives. Instead, they are usually marked by competing goals, personal and political conflict, time pressures, confusion, turbulence, ambiguity, misinformation, prejudices, and other complexities. This environment has led to such popular analogies as garbage cans and anarchies

NEW DIRECTIONS FOR INSTITUTIONAL RESEARCH, no. 67, Fall 1990 © Jossey-Bass Inc., Publishers

(March and Olsen, 1976), turbulent streams (Burns, 1978), patterns in streams (Mintzberg, 1978), and mazes (Simon, 1979).

In principle we all may endorse the ideals of rationality: "consistent, value maximizing choice within specified constraints" (Allison, 1971, p. 30) or "deciding what is correct behavior by relating consequences systematically to objectives" (March, 1976, p. 70). But we also recognize (as do Allison and March) that many situations do not neatly fit models of theoretically conceived rationality. In fact, institutions of higher education are often cited as prime examples of organizations that have difficulty making decisions rationally (Cyert and March, 1963; Chaffee, 1983). Simply put, the problem for colleges and universities becomes one of making decisions, allocating resources, and working toward goals in a theoretically imperfect world. In short, we need bridges between organization theory and the real-world practice of management. Strategic planning can help to build such bridges.

This chapter reviews The Pennsylvania State University's experience with planning over the past two decades. That experience has, on balance, been quite positive. This does not imply that it was necessarily the best way to manage a college or university or that it was even the best way to manage this particular institution. There is no absolute standard which allows one to say that a particular planning process has succeeded or failed.

Because the circumstances facing even a single institution change significantly over time, this chapter describes a planning and budgeting process that has evolved during the past twenty years. Flexibility, adaptation, individuality, responsiveness—these may be clichés in the management vocabulary, but their message is important. No single planning tool is right for all situations.

It is not our intent here to present a formula for successful planning. Rather, the Penn State experience is offered as an illustration of common principles that undergird every planning process and how they have come into play for one public research university since the early 1970s. But the principles are not unique to a particular institution or institutional type. The following account establishes a frame of reference for this case study.

The Evolution of Strategy in Higher Education

This chapter concentrates on the ways in which American colleges and universities have been managed over the past twenty years or so. It places the evolution of strategy during those years into four phases: horizontal reduction, vertical reallocation, strategic planning, and strategic management.

Phase One: Horizontal Reduction. Higher education in the United States flourished during the 1950s and 1960s in an essentially nurturing environment that encouraged broad growth. That situation abruptly changed in the early 1970s—what Chaffee (1984) calls a "shift point" for higher education—when economic, demographic, and political forces combined to alter the hospitable circumstances that many colleges and universities had enjoyed. Suddenly higher education heard a chorus of strident voices clamoring about retrenchment, stringency, uncertainty, reduction, and decline.

It was in the early 1970s that many campuses moved from a state of growth to one of, at best, stability. The predominant theme (Boulding, 1975; Mortimer and Tierney, 1979) became the management of decline, and the initial response of many institutions was to hold the line or reduce expenditures horizontally—that is, to make across-the-board cuts. By freezing positions, collapsing vacant positions, and cutting budgets, administrators attempted to forestall the possibility of radical changes such as merger, consolidation, or closure. In the early 1970s, these threats were quite real. Institutions closed their doors at an average rate of eighteen per year from 1968 to 1975, compared to about six closures annually in the early 1960s and again in the 1980s (National Center for Education Statistics, 1988).

Phase Two: Vertical Reallocation. Around 1975, the dialogue on many campuses and in the literature broadened to include a greater future orientation and the enhancement of institutional flexibility. Vertical reallocation—holding down expenditure growth while making selective choices about institutions and programs—became the foundation of differentially applied budget reallocations in the late 1970s and early 1980s (Carnegie Foundation, 1975; Lozier and Althouse, 1983). The emphasis in this second phase shifted from across-the-board reduction to reallocation and the setting of priorities as ways of dealing with financial stress.

Phase Three: Strategic Planning. The third phase, strategic planning, marks the transition from an internally focused, closed system (the traditional long-range plan) to an externally oriented, open system. This represents a quantum leap from earlier approaches. This third stage is anticipatory. The institution relies upon such concepts as definition of mission, environmental monitoring, and assessment of internal strengths and weaknesses to establish direction and guide decision processes and the search for appropriate niches in a larger environment. Strategic planning is, by definition, a systematic effort to define and possibly alter the organization's identity. The idea of strategic planning gained popularity in higher education with the publication of Keller's (1983) volume on academic strategy. That propitiously timed book, arriving on the heels of the popular *In Search of Excellence* (Peters and Waterman, 1982), found a ready audience at colleges and universities across the country.

Phase Four: Strategic Management. The concept of strategic management emerged from the 1970s business literature and has been defined as a "management process or system . . . that links strategic planning and decision-making with the day-to-day business of operational management" (Gluck, Kaufman, and Walleck, 1982, p. 10). In the third phase, strategic planning, organizations are thinking strategically, evaluating alternatives, allocating resources dynamically, and orienting management externally. In the fourth phase, these characteristics are integrated into the everyday management of the institution.

This distinction can be illustrated by considering the typical university strategic planning model, in which planning occurs at two levels. At the first level (probably the president's office), decisions are made about the entire university as a corporate body. At the second level, major planning units (such as individual schools) concentrate on their own environments and strategy development. Inherent in such a process is a powerful tendency toward compartmentalization. Strategic management is an effort to overcome this tendency by ensuring that participation in planning, as well as commitment to the precepts of strategic action, cut across all levels. Strategic management attempts to link all elements of planning (articulation of mission, goal formulation, strategy development, and so on) with the nuts and bolts of running the institution. Not surprisingly, few organizations attain such a thorough integration of planning and management (Gluck, Kaufman, and Walleck, 1980).

The Case Study

This case describes how, from 1970 through 1989, The Pennsylvania State University adapted the decision-making processes it uses for planning and resource allocation. Over that period, the university progressed through the first three of the four phases described above. The institution is continuing the process of adjusting and redirecting its planning processes.

Today Penn State enrolls 70,000 students at a network of twenty-two campuses across the Commonwealth of Pennsylvania. Approximately 37,000 students are located at the University Park campus, 24,000 at seventeen two-year feeder campuses, and the remainder at such locations as the medical school and upper-division/graduate campuses. The university has a corporate charter and is "state related" as opposed to being state owned. Penn State receives a smaller share of its budget from state appropriations than most public institutions (about 21 percent of the total budget and 41 percent of the general funds budget) and has a high degree of management autonomy. The university has a 1989-90 budget of over $1 billion.

The year 1970 saw the end of an era for Penn State. During a single presidential administration, from 1956 to 1970, the university experienced rapid overall growth. The student population nearly tripled in size (from 17,000 to 48,000), the faculty nearly doubled in size (from 1,600 to 3,000), and the total annual budget quintupled (from $34 million to $177 million). This expansion was supported with generously growing state appropriations. Increases for 1965-66 through 1969-70 were 21 percent, 31 percent, 22 percent, 22 percent, and 17 percent.

The 1970s, however, brought the beginning of a general economic recession that hit Pennsylvania hard, and the state went from record budget surpluses to near-bankruptcy. By the late 1970s, state appropriation growth had slowed markedly. Increases for 1976–77 through 1980–81 were 4 percent, zero, 5 percent, 7 percent, and 8 percent. Through the 1970s, unavoidable increases in retirement and Social Security costs, medical insurance, and fuel and utilities expenses far outpaced increases in state funding and resulted in rapid tuition increases. In addition, since 1970 Penn State has been trying to cope with substantial enrollment increases. From 1970–71 to 1989–90 Penn State's enrollment climbed by 40 percent.

The external turbulence facing the institution was exacerbated by fundamental shifts within the university as well. From 1971 to 1981, for example, the percentage of students enrolled in engineering rose from 11 percent to 18 percent of total enrollment while the percentage of students enrolled in education declined from 15 percent to 7 percent.

Over the past twenty years, Penn State's approach to management and resource allocation has gone through four phases: horizontal reduction, vertical reallocation, strategic planning, and issue management. Each of these stages is described in the sections that follow.

Horizontal Reduction: 1971–1976. The initial response of Penn State to the stringency of the early 1970s was to reduce or hold the line on expenditures horizontally. From 1971 through 1976, the university utilized annual across-the-board budget reductions for all units. It was looking for savings through position freezes, the collapse of vacant positions, and decremental budgeting. Although horizontal reduction can in some situations be an effective short-term tactic, internal pressures shifted substantially over that five-year period—for example, enrollments in the College of Business increased by 1,500 students while enrollments in Education declined by about the same number. In the face of such changes, Penn State's administrators realized that continued proportional budget cuts for all units at some point would become unsound and irresponsible.

Vertical Reallocation: 1977–1982. In 1977 the university adopted a rolling five-year budget planning process based upon differentially applied internal reallocations. This approach still aimed at holding down overall expenditure growth, but it permitted bolder decisions about the resources distributed to individual units. Under this program, from 1977 through 1982, the average budget cut for all academic units was 4.7 percent, but budget decisions ranged from increases of over 20 percent to a cut of 12.5 percent. The focus of the process was on reallocation through careful medium-range planning (Lozier and Althouse, 1983). This approach was characteristic of how campuses were responding to stringency at the time.

Strategic Planning: 1983–1988. During the periods of horizontal reduction and vertical reallocation, Penn State had initiated two conventional master planning processes that paved the way for strategic planning.

The Academic Policy Plan (Pennsylvania State University, 1972), adopted by the board of trustees in July 1972, described a university accustomed to rapid growth in the 1960s entering a period of comparative stringency. This document assessed the university's current status and pointed out a number of continuing problems. In 1978, the board of trustees authorized an update of *The Academic Policy Plan* and, in January 1980, received *A Perspective on the '80s: An Agenda for Action* (Pennsylvania State University, 1980). Like the earlier document, the *Perspective* provided a well-written assessment of the university's strengths and weaknesses as it entered a new decade. Although a number of its recommendations were carried out, the perception throughout the university was generally one of indifference and a sense that little change would result. The *Perspective,* in spite of its title, was not the catalyst for a great deal of action. In fact, because of a generally negative attitude toward planning on campus, the use of the word *plan* anywhere in the document was deliberately avoided.

In 1983, Penn State entered the third phase of institutional response: implementing a comprehensive program of strategic planning. The process retained the concept of selectively reallocating resources internally. But compared to earlier planning processes, strategic planning has been more externally oriented, more explicit about the university's long-range aspirations, more emphatic about building upon strengths, and more committed to a participatory process for addressing cross-organizational issues. Finally, since 1984 strategic planning has been linked to the university's ongoing budgeting process—thereby correcting a severe shortcoming of the master planning efforts of the previous decade.

In establishing the strategic planning program at the initiation of the president, the board of trustees stated that the process would be driven by the need to set "priorities . . . likely to propel The Pennsylvania State University to a place among the best comprehensive, public universities of the nation" (Pennsylvania State University, 1984, p. 1). This aspiration is quite different from the essentially defensive goal—minimizing the erosion of important programs and units—of the earlier phases of recycling and reduction.

The strategic planning process took an external, open-systems approach that was very much based on the theme of building upon existing strengths. To facilitate this end, the president appointed a strategic planning advisory committee composed mostly of faculty members with long experience in leadership roles as department heads, assistant deans, and faculty senators. The charge to the committee was basically to develop a "plan to plan." Based largely on the work of that committee, and with extensive support from the staff of the planning office, in 1984 the office of the president issued the *Strategic Planning Guide.* This document described the purpose of strategic planning at Penn State, outlined how the process would work, and provided individual units such as colleges with principles to guide their planning efforts. The guide indicated that strategic planning would be an evolutionary process and that adjustments would be made annually to incorporate both internal and external changes. Each fall from 1985 through 1988 an update to the guide was issued by the office of the president. Using this framework, both Penn State as a whole and each college and major administrative unit of the university initiated a systematic and ongoing evaluation of strengths and weaknesses, opportunities and threats.

Specially appointed strategic study groups—with heavy representation of faculty with disciplinary expertise in relevant fields such as economics, demography, and technology—have been used to address planning issues that cross organizational boundaries. In August 1984, for example, the president appointed a strategic study group to analyze the feasibility of creating a School of Communications at Penn State. At the time, elements of mass communications were contained in at least four of the university's colleges (Liberal Arts, Arts and Architecture, Education, and Agriculture) and in the university's television and radio stations. The study group was chaired by the long-time administrator of the university's telecommunications services, who was also a faculty member in journalism. Most members of the group were faculty from departments likely to be most affected by the creation of the new school, along with a few faculty from other disciplines and staff support from the planning office.

In October 1984 the study group submitted its report to the president, strongly endorsing the creation of a School of Communications and discussing the strengths and weaknesses of six alternative configurations for such a unit. During 1984-85, the president and his staff continued to work toward the creation of the new school by developing financial projections and meeting with various constituencies such as college deans, faculty senate committees, and the board of trustees. The board approved the creation of the School of Communications, the first major academic reorganization at Penn State in almost twenty years. (For a detailed description of this case see Lozier, Dooris, and Chittipeddi, 1986.)

The School of Communications study group was among the first of many study groups that were used to deal with strategic issues which crossed organizational boundaries. A similar approach was used, for example, to study the creation of a new College of Health and Human Development, once again involving departments in several colleges, to study the establishment of a comprehensive employee wellness program involving academic units such as nutrition and nursing as well as administrative units such as the office of human resources, and to study faculty development encompassing individual, departmental, and administrative roles and responsibilities.

In addition to such ad hoc committees, the strategic planning process has directly linked strategic planning priorities to resource allocation decisions. This has been accomplished by developing a process that combines discussion of each unit's strategic plan—the assessment of strengths and weaknesses, statement of mission and goals, and so on—with the analysis of resource needs and the allocation of budgets. This process is based upon strategic plans written or updated by each unit every year and upon annual committee hearings, chaired by the provost, at which strategies are analyzed and budget priorities set.

Penn State has had five years' experience with this strategic planning procedure (1984-85 through 1988-89). A vital ingredient in the process has been the strategic enhancement of selected programs through differential allocation of resources, ultimately the responsibility of the provost and president. In addition to guiding reallocation decisions for existing units, strategic planning has resulted in major initiatives:

- Creation of a new School of Communications
- Creation of a new Biotechnology Institute
- Establishment of a new College of Health and Human Development through realignment of programs from three colleges
- Completion of the university's first major capital campaign
- Termination of the department and program in community studies and reallocation of those resources to other units
- Establishment of a Division of Technology within the feeder system of branch campuses
- Initiation of a two-year comprehensive study on the status of women at the university
- Reorganization of numerous other administrative and academic operations (student services and academic support programs, computing and information systems, research and the graduate school).

But establishing, terminating, and reorganizing are only means, not ends in themselves. Reasonable people may well ask if anything has truly changed as a result of strategic planning.

We cannot know, of course, where Penn State would be today had different paths been taken. Moreover, many of the initiatives undertaken through the mechanism of strategic planning are truly long-term in nature and their outcomes are difficult to gauge at present. Nevertheless, we believe that the university has been able to progress more rapidly within the strategic planning framework than it would have done under prior administrative processes and that the university has in fact advanced toward its strategic goal of being one of the country's top public research universities. The capital campaign—one of the five largest public university fund-raising drives ever—has succeeded beyond expectations. The target of $300 million was met with six months remaining in the campaign, and the university increased the number of endowed faculty positions from just 19 to

110. From 1984 to 1989, graduate enrollments increased by 26 percent, minority enrollments increased by 70 percent, the number of minority faculty increased by 70 percent, and the number of female faculty increased by one-third. Expenditures on research and development have nearly doubled, and the university has advanced in virtually every national ranking of research funding. In December 1989, Penn State accepted an invitation to join the Big Ten conference, thereby affiliating with some of the most prestigious research universities in the country. These and other indicators of progress were not all the result of specific strategic choices, of course. But taken together they clearly suggest that the university has moved toward its strategic goals over the past six years.

The evaluation of specific academic reorganizations is more subjective and requires a longer time horizon, but here again the signs are positive. As noted, the creation of the School of Communications in 1985 was the first such change resulting from strategic planning and provides at least a limited opportunity for assessment. Penn State's journalism/mass communication program has, under the egis of the new school, grown from twenty-fifth to second in the nation in terms of size, has been glowingly reaccredited, and has attracted outstanding students and faculty members. The problems accompanying the creation of the school—such as the need for controls on the number of entering students and for substantial improvements in space and facilities—have largely come about because the initiatives met or surpassed its initial goals much more quickly than anticipated. Few on campus would argue that the first major academic reorganization at Penn State since the 1950s is shaping up as anything short of success.

Issue Management: 1990 and Beyond. Thus far in the discussion, the Penn State case study has followed closely the first three phases in the evolution of planning: horizontal reduction, vertical reallocation, and strategic planning. The fourth stage, strategic management, is the combination of strategic planning and management into a single process. Penn State has not yet reached that level but is currently moving in that direction by developing an issue management program. This label communicates more distinctly than "strategic management" a set of goals and processes that build upon but are different from the strategic planning process used over the past five years. The goals of issue management at Penn State are described below but in essence they are twofold: to encourage planning involvement at all levels of the organization and to focus attention upon themes important to the university as a whole. In effect, issue management is a call to think globally and act locally.

As a prelude to entering this new phase, during the 1988-89 academic year the provost of the university and the executive director of planning initiated a series of discussions with deans, other key executives, and faculty senate leaders to evaluate strategic planning. Not surprisingly, some problems were identified. These included insufficient funding to address legitimate needs and unrealistic expectations that accompanied the strategic planning thrust, a problem discussed below. On balance, however, the appraisal of the overall process resulted in an overwhelming endorsement. In particular, Penn State's executives viewed the use of study groups to tackle cross-organizational issues as a major strength of strategic planning. In accordance with that assessment, the university is now revamping the planning process to focus explicitly on strategic issues and to require individual units to address these issues in their strategic plans.

Strategic issues can be defined as critical policy questions that frame the fundamental choices faced by an organizational unit—the university, a college, a department, a campus, or a support area. (For a comprehensive discussion of strategic issue identification and its role in strategy formulation, see Bryson, 1988.) Issue management at Penn State is to be particularly attuned to themes of strategic importance to the university as a whole, such as promoting diversity or addressing long-term needs for physical facilities. It is less driven by considerations specific to individual units such as changing demand for particular programs. But along with this emphasis on overall direction, the process is designed to further integrate planning, both horizontally and vertically, by deeply involving all academic and administrative units in the identification of issues of shared importance. The issue management rubric is being used to balance a greater sensitivity to university-level considerations with grass-roots involvement in shaping the agenda of the common cause.

As Penn State enters the 1990s, the groundwork for achieving that delicate balance is being laid. In September 1989 two one-day strategic planning seminars were conducted for academic deans, associate deans, department heads, university vice-presidents and directors, campus executive officers, the University Faculty Senate leadership and Committee on Academic and Physical Planning, and student government leadership. The focus of the seminars was on the definition and management of strategic issues. From these sessions a preliminary set of strategic issues emerged, including student demographics, state funding, and faculty supply and demand. During the fall of 1989 considerable consultation was conducted with all these groups, which in turn consulted with their respective constituencies.

The planning office crystallized that consultation into a written set of strategic issues. These issues included the university's long-term space and facilities needs, concerns about diversity, and other themes of importance to the university as a whole. This set of issues was then discussed widely throughout Penn State. The provost asked units to incorporate these university-level issues into the plans and resource requests submitted in the fall of 1990 as input to the planning and budgeting process for 1991-92. These unit plans will be evaluated by the university's planning and budgeting committee to see how well they address these university-wide issues. Based on the ideas presented in the unit draft plans, a revised overall statement of the university's direction will be centrally prepared during 1990–91 with involvement of the planning staff and broad consultation. That statement will address the strategic issues set forth in the fall of 1989.

Planning Principles

The following sections draw upon the Penn State experience, and upon our understanding of the literature, to develop a set of operational principles about university planning:

- Debate about whether planning works is less helpful than careful consideration of *how* it should be conceived and applied.
- Given the meager resources typically available for discretionary allocation, expect change to occur on the margins.
- Planning requires time and continuity.
- Because dollars are limited, other forms of feedback are important.
- Planning is likely to be resisted and therefore ineffective if begun during a period of serious retrenchment.
- Excessive paperwork and shelf documents sap time, energy, and interest.
- Planning occurs within political constraints that must be recognized.
- To improve the chances of initial success, start small. The scope of planning is less important than breadth of involvement and acceptance through the organization.

Not Whether But How. Observers have pointed out a number of pitfalls that often accompany strategic planning. Schmidtlein and Milton (1989) have described, we believe very accurately, the dissatisfaction that has marked strategic planning programs at some colleges and universities. Their review of planning experiences at a sample of institutions across the United States concluded that there is a considerable gap between the literature's optimistic prescriptions and the cynicism, resistance, and confusion that often accompany campus planning.

On the other hand, a study comparable to Schmidtlein and Milton's reached different conclusions about participants' satisfaction with strategic planning at their institutions. Meredith, Lenning, and Cope (1988) studied thirty-four institutions actively engaged in strategic planning. Based on responses from planning officers, academic vice-presidents, and presidents to twenty questions about the use of environmental scanning, the extent of planning at the departmental level, and other items, the institutions were classified on the basis of whether their process represented bona fide strategic planning. Respondents from institutions that engaged in bona fide planning reported greater satisfaction with the effort, and believed they were getting better results, than did counterparts at institutions doing less bona fide planning. The authors conclude: "We believe our results support those administrators (and some faculty activists) who have urged and adopted the strategic planning concept" (p. 10).

The disparity between these two findings is probably more apparent than real. As Gilmore and Lozier (1987) note: "The problems often found with strategic planning applications—over-fragmentation, paper driven, control oriented, mechanistic and modeling dependent, and failure to account for organizational culture and constituency groups—are more the results of how we apply strategic planning principles than with the basic constructs themselves" (p. 21). In short, the literature suggests that the question of whether planning works may be less appropriate than *how*, in specific instances, planning is undertaken. This conclusion, while not a recommendation per se, is the justification for the principles that follow.

Change on the Margins. One of the problems with undertaking a highly visible strategic planning program is that expectations may be raised beyond an institution's means. At Penn State, the administration can allocate only $5 or $6 million per year in new permanent funding, out of a total annual budget of over $1 billion, to strategic initiatives put forth by unit heads. The bulk of budget increases must instead support salaries, Social Security, retirement and insurance expenses, facilities maintenance, and the like. Does this mean that strategic planning cannot have an impact? We think not. An exemplary study by Clugston (1988) examined whether strategic planning affected resource allocation decisions at a large midwestern university. Clugston's regression results showed small but significant effects in which strategic priorities explained about 3 percent of the variation in budget allocations to departments. He concluded that strategic planning does make a difference.

It is not surprising that the magnitude of the effect reported by Clugston was basically on the margin, given the relatively small portion of funds typically available for discretionary allocation. This does not imply that a shift of 3 percent is unimportant. Even modest changes are cumulative. Decisions about discretionary funds or the reallocation of positions resulting from serendipitous departures are marginal changes, but in time they can help an institution in pursuit of a long-term vision. It has been helpful at Penn State to occasionally remind administrators and faculty that strategic planning does not, in itself, create any new funds and that much of its impact may not be immediately evident.

Continuity. One of the critics quoted in the Schmidtlein and Milton (1989, p. 15) study was a president who spoke of the benefits of a recently completed planning effort. When asked if he would repeat the exercise, however, he answered, "Never during the remainder of my tenure as president!" This response typifies the experience of many institutions that have undertaken one or two major planning cycles. But according to an important school of thought in organizational decision making, continuity and a longer perspective are necessary to any management approach.

Quinn's (1980) work combines theory with examples drawn from business and government to make a convincing case for what he calls "logical incrementalism." Quinn argues that successful management is often tentative, gradual, flexible, open to feedback and change, and adaptive. For that reason, Quinn believes that major changes in strategy must emerge and evolve over time. Scott (1981, p. 281) makes a similar point about the importance of permitting "experiential learning"—the idea that while managers start out with broad goals, those goals (along with strategies to achieve them) must be allowed to evolve and adapt.

Both the literature and our own experience with master planning efforts indicate that one-shot planning is not likely to produce more than the proverbial shelf document. Planning is a learning tool. It is evolutionary and its impact occurs gradually. It is built on awareness, on the dissemination of information throughout the organization, on building on ideas that work, and on discarding or modifying ideas that do not. Planning requires a continuity of people and experiences. It takes time.

Feedback. The previous two points—the notions that change occurs on the margin and that continuity is important—lead to a discussion about the importance of feedback to unit heads such as deans and vice-presidents. Dollars are concrete, but progress toward institutional goals is often intangible. Cynicism about a planning process thrives on a lack of formal feedback about the status of goals and priorities. When Penn State carried out its five-year assessment of planning, one dean pointed out the need for more explicit comment on the intellectual directions and ambitions set forth by unit plans and on specific goals that might not have received funding but otherwise have the endorsement of the university's leadership. Formal feedback should not be limited to the approval or denial of budget requests.

Planning and Retrenchments. Planning should not be introduced in the face of major adversity. Although some might argue that a strategic approach is most important at such times, there is already a built-in cynicism about planning in general. If planning is undertaken at a time of serious retrenchment, this cynicism is likely to grow. Also, many administrators will in essence refuse to play when they are asked to say where their own budgets should be cut. In the mid 1970s, Penn State asked all administrators what they would eliminate as the result of a hypothetical 6 percent reduction in their unit's budget. Most responses suggested clearly impossible cuts to vital programs or services.

An established planning program with a record of success can perhaps be used as a tool for retrenchment. However, planning is less likely to succeed if it is begun in response to a pressing need for major reductions.

Paperwork and Shelf Documents. Two warnings about planning relate to the creation of paperwork. First, campuses should avoid a forms-driven process that saps time, energy, and interest. Second, campuses should avoid producing a plan that is merely a shelf document. These two points are based on what planning should and should not be. Bryson (1988) defines strategic planning as a disciplined effort to shape what an organization is and does. The emphasis of planning should be on decisions and action. Forms and master plans can be very informative about what an organization *was*. And communication, decision making, and feedback in a college or university do require reports, studies, and memoranda. Expect a planning process to generate paper, but do not let this obscure the fact that planning is not about what the organization was but what it will become.

Political Constraints. Any college or university initiating planning does so in a political context. At Penn State, a planning and budgeting process was in place. The process worked and was accepted. It is necessary to build upon the existing resource allocation structure and procedures.

Also, a college or university may already have standing committees on such matters as academic and physical planning. When strategic planning is undertaken, the composition, strength, and potential contribution of these groups must be assessed carefully in determining whether and how they will be used.

The importance of leadership need not be discussed here in detail. The literature and our experience are consistent: The support of the president and chief academic officer can make or break strategic planning. The process at Penn State was undertaken in 1983 at the initiative of the president and succeeded only because of his continuing commitment.

Starting Small. A comprehensive strategic planning effort (as described by Bryson, 1988) that deals with mission, mandate, strengths, weaknesses, opportunities, threats, and so on may be beyond the reach of many institutions, at least initially. If so, planners should reduce the scope of planning rather than cut back on the breadth of involvement across the organization. All units, academic and administrative, should be included. If strategic planning is to be accepted, everyone in the organization must believe they have an opportunity to participate and benefit in some way.

Starting small may also be advantageous to the extent that it enables an institution to build political support on the basis of early accomplishments. The first major reorganization carried out through strategic planning at Penn State was the creation of the School of Communications, which at the time involved about 30 faculty and 800 students. The attention paid to this change within the university was intense compared to later strategic reorganizations. The highly visible success of the School of Communications probably contributed to the relative ease with which the creation of a much larger unit, the new College of Health and Human Development, with about 225 faculty and 3,000 students, was accomplished two years later.

Role of Institutional Research

According to Boyles (1988), in the 1960s and early 1970s the emphasis of institutional research (IR) was on enrollment data, faculty workload, self-studies, external reporting, and the like. In the later 1970s and the 1980s, responsibilities centered on the "analysis of evolving policy issues" and "management, advocacy, and policy research" (Boyles, 1988, p. 199). IR functions, and even the titles of IR positions and offices, are being expanded to encompass planning in some way. How should IR professionals approach this role?

Marvin Hagler, former middleweight champion of the world, describes himself by saying, "I am a fighter who walks, talks, and thinks fighting, but I try not to look like it." While Hagler's appearance may or may not be deceiving, his idea can serve those with planning responsibilities. Whether that person is the chief planning officer, the director of IR, or an IR staffer, the role should be clearly defined as that of a facilitator—not as "the planner" of the college or university. Instead, every dean, department head, director, and manager in the organization must be seen as a planner.

A planning process does need someone to conceptualize, coordinate, monitor, and support it. Someone must collect information, provide consistent reporting definitions, conduct analyses, produce data packages, and write reports. While these functions are typically carried out by IR/planning personnel, as they are at Penn State, it may also be desirable to use faculty resources via released time. This approach might seem most necessary at colleges with very limited IR resources, but it can also be productive in other situations. At Penn State, for example, an associate professor of sociology on released time served as research director of a study on the status of women at Penn State and worked with virtually the entire staff of the planning office. This was a subject in which he had particular expertise and an ongoing research interest. The appointment worked to the mutual benefit of the IR staff and the faculty member and clearly enhanced the quality of the study.

This chapter is based on the implicit assumption that planning can work in colleges and universities. The evidence we have seen supports that assumption. Planning can draw on a variety of formal models. Carefully crafted and patiently applied, planning can succeed. And as the IR role expands to include planning responsibilities, practitioners will benefit from an awareness of work being done in management, decision making, organization theory, and related fields, as well as at other colleges and universities. The literature does not have all the answers, but it can provide an indispensable portfolio of ideas and experiences about formal approaches to planning.

References

Allison, G. T. *Essence of Decision*. Boston: Little, Brown, 1971.

Boulding, K. E. "The Management of Decline." *Change*, 1975, *64*, 8–9.

Boyles, C. V. "Help Wanted: A Profile of Institutional Research, 1970–1985." *Research in Higher Education*, 1988, *28* (3), 195–216.

Bryson, J. M. *Strategic Planning for Public and Nonprofit Organizations*. San Francisco: Jossey-Bass, 1988.

Burns, J. M. *Leadership*. New York: Harper & Row, 1978.

Carnegie Foundation for the Advancement of Teaching. *More Than Survival: Proposals for Higher Education in a Period of Uncertainty*. San Francisco: Jossey-Bass, 1975.

Chaffee, E. E. "Rationality in University Budgeting." *Research in Higher Education*, 1983, *19* (4), 387–406.

Chaffee, E. E. *After Decline, What? Survival Strategies at Eight Private Colleges*. Boulder, Colo.: National Center for Higher Education Management Systems, 1984.

Clugston, R. M. "Strategic Adaptation in Organized Anarchy: Priority Setting and Resource Allocation in the Liberal Arts College of a Public Research University." Washington, D.C.: American Association of University Administrators Foundation, 1988.

Cyert, R. M., and March, J. G. *A Behavioral Theory of the Firm*. Englewood Cliffs, N.J.: Prentice-Hall, 1963.

Gilmore, J. L., and Lozier, G. G. "Managing Strategic Planning: A Systems Theory Approach." *Educational Planning*, 1987, *6* (1), 12–23.

Gluck, F. W., Kaufman, S. P., and Walleck, A. S. "Strategic Management for Competitive Advantage." *Harvard Business Review*, 1980, *58* (4), 154–161.

Gluck, F. W., Kaufman, S. P., and Walleck, A. S. "The Four Phases of Strategic Management." *Journal of Business Strategy*, 1982, *2* (3), 9–21.

Keller, G. A. *Academic Strategy*. Baltimore and London: Johns Hopkins University Press, 1983.

Lozier, G. G., and Althouse, P. R. "Developing Planning and Budgeting Strategies for Internal Recycling of Funds." *Research in Higher Education*, 1983, *18* (2), 237–250.

Lozier, G. G., Dooris, M. J., and Chittipeddi, K. "A Case Study in Issues Management." *Planning for Higher Education*, 1986, *14* (4), 14–19.

March, J. G. "The Technology of Foolishness." In J. G. March and J. P. Olsen (eds.), *Ambiguity and Choice in Organizations*. Bergen, Norway: Universitetsforlaget, 1976.

March, J. G., and Olsen, J. P. *Ambiguity and Choice in Organizations*. Bergen, Norway: Universitetsforlaget, 1976.

Meredith, M., Lenning, O., and Cope, R. "After Six Years, Does Strategic Planning Matter?" Paper presented at the Association of Institutional Research Forum, Phoenix, Ariz., May 15–18, 1988.

Mintzberg, H. "Patterns in Strategy Formulation." *Management Science*, 1978, *24* (9), 934–948.

Mortimer, K. P., and Tierney, M. L. *The Three "R's" of the Eighties: Reduction, Reallocation, and Retrenchment*. AAHE-ERIC/Higher Education Research Report No. 4. Washington, D.C.: American Association for Higher Education, 1979.

National Center for Education Statistics. *Digest of Education Statistics 1988*. Washington, D.C.: Government Printing Office, September 1988.

Pennsylvania State University. *The Academic Policy Plan*. University Park, Pa.: Office of the President, 1972.

Pennsylvania State University. *Perspective on the '80s: An Agenda for Action*. University Park, Pa.: Office of the President, 1980.

Pennsylvania State University. *Strategic Planning Guide*. University Park, Pa.: Office of the President, 1984.

Peters, T. J., and Waterman, R. H. *In Search of Excellence: Lessons from America's Best-Run Companies*. New York: Harper & Row, 1982.

Quinn, J. B. *Strategies for Change: Logical Incrementalism*. Homewood, Ill.: Irwin, 1980.

Schmidtlein, F. A., and Milton, T. H. "Campus Planning in the United States: Perspectives from a Nation-Wide Study." *Planning for Higher Education*, 1989, *17* (3), 1–19.

Scott, W. R. *Organizations: Rational, Natural, and Open Systems*. Englewood Cliffs, N.J.: Prentice-Hall, 1981.

Simon, H. A. *Models of Thought*. New Haven, Conn.: Yale University Press, 1979.

Michael J. Dooris is senior planning analyst in planning and analysis at The Pennsylvania State University.

G. Gregory Lozier is executive director of planning and analysis at The Pennsylvania State University and a member of the graduate faculty in higher education.

Many formal planning processes simply refine the status quo.
Entrepreneurial planning at a private university achieved significant
change.

Entrepreneurial Planning: Tufts University

John A. Dunn, Jr.

Under the leadership of President Jean Mayer, Tufts University's planning over the last fourteen years can best be characterized as entrepreneurial— seeking out opportunities for significant advances whose potential gains justify the risks and investments involved. This chapter focuses on several key strategic decisions taken at Tufts during this period, with a particular emphasis on identifying the role played by formal planning and institutional research.

While this entrepreneurial approach to planning has, by and large, worked well at Tufts in this period, it is clearly not appropriate for all institutions in all situations. It is more effective in changing institutions than in refining them. It requires astute, aggressive leadership and a great deal of decision-making autonomy. It creates risks and wrenches the status quo. In general, it is of interest because it is not the consensus-building, formalized, constituency-based approach to planning that is often recommended.

The reader should keep in mind that the view presented here is through a particular pair of eyes. The author cannot pretend to objectivity, having been directly involved in the decision making and implementation throughout the period. Moreover, this chapter is written with the wisdom of hindsight. What now seems compelling in its logic often seemed a leap of faith at the time. What seems now to be a sensible risk (because it worked) caused a considerable shaking of heads at the outset. Apparently unrelated actions are

The author wishes to thank Senior Vice-President Thomas W. Murnane, Executive Vice-President Steven S. Manos, Provost Sol Gittleman, and Board Secretary Joseph J. Lambert for their careful reading and helpful critique of the manuscript.

now seen—correctly or not—to have formed a coherent pattern. Nonetheless, useful lessons can perhaps be drawn. Was it Kierkegaard who said that one lives life forward but only understands it backward?

After a brief discussion of the general nature of strategic decisions, we turn to Tufts University as incoming President Jean Mayer found it in 1976 and the strategies he and his colleagues employed to strengthen it. The chapter then considers an overall description of Tufts' present planning and priority-setting process and concludes with an evaluation of the role played by formal planning and institutional research.

Strategic Decisions and Institutional Change

Strategic decisions are those key decisions in the life of an institution that shape its character and determine its place in the environment. Some strategic decisions are made consciously and are highly visible—as in the case of starting a major new school or moving to a new campus. Others can be understood only in retrospect, since they were made over the course of several years and implemented incrementally. Such a case might be found in the gradual growth of a school's vocational programs to compensate for a slowly shrinking liberal arts market. Strategic decisions can be made internally, as in the case of a decision to change pricing policy to appeal to a different audience, or externally, as when a state system assigns a new mission to a campus.

There are few strategic decisions taken in the life of a university president. Indeed, an institution that serves a continuing market with stable programs, with student charges and financial aid policies that move with its peer group, and with fund raising and construction that continue at a normal pace, can be said to be making only one strategic decision: to stay in its market.

While strategic decisions may be few, they are of critical importance. If such a decision is well made—that is, if the institution accurately perceives a significant need and undertakes to provide a service that fulfills it—it has a high likelihood of success, barring stupid implementation or some extraordinary change in environment. If the decisions are made badly, on the other hand, no amount of tactical planning can raise the probability of success.

Strategic decisions involve getting the few big things right, rather than having lots of data. They tend to be intuitive, value driven, and based on a clear understanding of the nature of the enterprise and what can be accomplished, given the world in which it operates. Tactical and operational planning, in contrast, involve shorter time frames, are more focused on events and people within the institution, and often require more extensive and more precise data. As shown in this case study, formal planning and institutional research are more helpful at the tactical planning level than at the strategic level. To draw out these lessons, we need to look first at the university as President Mayer found it and, in that context, at the strategic decisions he made.

The Setting

Tufts University is an independent nonsectarian institution founded in 1852 by the Universalist Church. In 1976, when Mayer took office, Tufts enrolled a total of 6,500 students in undergraduate Liberal Arts and Engineering colleges, a range of master's and doctoral programs, the Fletcher School of Law and Diplomacy, and first-professional programs in medicine and dental medicine. The Arts and Sciences programs were carried on at a suburban campus in Medford and Somerville, Massachusetts, and the health sciences in Boston. Tufts was classified in the Carnegie Commission scheme as a Research University II, although its production of doctorates and its research activity barely merited that ranking.

Tufts' programs were ambitious for its resources; endowment income and unrestricted gifts together only accounted for 4 percent of total revenues. Student charges in all programs were among the highest nationally. Library resources were at the level of a good college rather than a university, and computing support was modest at best. Tufts' strengths, however, were real. It had a faculty dedicated to excellence in teaching, a strong admissions appeal, a worldwide reputation for the Fletcher School, and strong clinical faculties in medicine and dental medicine. It was an agreeable place to work with people dedicated to the institution and to each other.

During the late 1950s and early 1960s, President Nils Wessell had raised Tufts' ambitions. He hiked faculty salaries, started a number of master's and doctoral programs, recruited students from a far wider geographic area, eliminated several vocationally oriented programs, and started an "Experimental College." To symbolize new directions, he changed the institution's name from Tufts College to Tufts University. Burton Hallowell, president during the late 1960s and early 1970s, initiated several additional curricular reforms, pursued the raising of faculty standards, but cut back on some of the graduate programs that Tufts did not have the resources to do well. To his credit, Hallowell brought Tufts relatively unscathed through that difficult period of rapid inflation and student disruption.

Tufts in the middle 1970s could be characterized as an institution searching to be a distinguished university but lacking the resources to achieve that goal; as a university excellent in its teaching but unremarkable in its research; as one with the complexities of decentralized management and multiple campuses, heavily invested in the health sciences, miscellaneous in its graduate programs, comparatively small in enrollment, and for an institution with its set of programs, limited in its financial and facilities capital.

The Challenge

President Jean Mayer, taking office in 1976, wanted to advance the institution, to enhance its reputation, and to achieve both distinction and distinctiveness in its programs. Any new president, often before even arriving permanently on campus, examines the institution to see what levers he or she may employ to move it in the desired direction. The most important internal resource for enhancement, of course, is the faculty. President Wessell had signaled the need to add scholarship and research emphases to what had been mostly a teaching faculty. That shift continued under Hallowell, but there were limits to what could be done. Since Tufts had a student-faculty ratio of about 16 to 1, not even the best faculty had much time for research and scholarship. The faculty, though improving in their research capabilities, were by and large not major grant-getters. Especially in the health sciences, where competitive funding through NIH is the key to development, the Tufts faculty (with a few exceptions) could not bring in major grants and therefore could not grow.

Another standard option for acquiring additional resources is to grow. Tufts had been following this path for several decades, adding about 150 students a year from 1950 through the late 1970s. Though there had been some new construction (especially of dormitories) during this period, the campus buildings were already full; any growth would require new facilities. Aggravating this difficulty was the fact that Tufts, like many other institutions, was not spending enough to keep its existing plant in good condition. Furthermore, the projected demographic decline for the 1980s made counting on major growth in enrollment questionable.

Financially, Tufts was sound but thin. Wessell and Hallowell had achieved balanced budgets in all but one year each. However, these operating budgets provided very little flexibility. Endowments totaled only $27 million and were heavily restricted as to use. There were few if any reserves.

The final traditional source of leverage for institutional advancement is fund raising. Tufts had, at best, an unimpressive record with two unsuccessful capital campaigns as its only ventures in twenty years. A university-wide campaign in the 1950s for a modest $7 million was acclaimed to have reached its goal but really produced only $4.5 million in usable support. A campaign for the School of Dental Medicine in the late 1960s again had a goal of $7 million but produced only about $4.5 million. Both campaigns achieved the desired numbers and dollars from givers of modest amounts, but they lacked the high-level leadership gifts. Many alumni were loyal to Tufts, but less than 20 percent were donating each year. Total annual fund-raising proceeds had risen from under $2 million in the 1960s to between $3 and $4 million in the early 1970s. President Hallowell had started planning a new capital campaign for the mid 1970s, but outside fund-raising counsel estimated its potential as being only about $20 to $25 million.

The essence of the challenge was how to achieve the desired distinction and distinctiveness with inadequate internal resources. This situation is not uncommon; in fact, many incoming presidents believe it is typical. A frequent response is to engage the campus leadership in a formal planning process. If a good committee, with direct or indirect leadership from the president, can build consensus around areas to be emphasized in the future, it can complement the president's actions in building his or her own team, raising standards for tenure, seeking a few key faculty appointments, using the budget process to channel resources, and raising funds for programs of special interest. The major advantage of this approach is that it minimizes campus conflict by making people feel included. The major disadvantages are that it is slow and the changes are apt to be refinements rather than significant shifts.

President Mayer wanted to move more quickly than such a committee process would have permitted. More important, he sought changes of a character that committees cannot usually contemplate.

Strategic Directions

The essence of Mayer's strategy was to acquire external resources to leverage the internal strengths. He and his senior colleagues identified programs of education and research that met several criteria: they were of intellectual interest and value in themselves; they were of sufficient importance to attract private and public support; and they complemented and enriched Tufts' existing programs.

Any reading of history is by nature selective. I have somewhat arbitrarily chosen six major strategic directions for discussion. Three of them are programmatic and directly fit the criteria just mentioned. The other three are more organizational in character and complement the programs. The first five were presidential initiatives; the last was an organizational necessity developed with his support. They were

- To develop a School of Veterinary Medicine complementing Tufts' strengths in the health sciences and meeting a New England need
- To develop a focus on nutrition at the university, anchored with a federally funded research center on nutrition and aging
- To link Tufts' engineering, public policy, and health sciences strengths through a major research focus on environmental management
- To infuse an entrepreneurial liberation into the institution, changing the signals for faculty members and administrators from an emphasis on teaching and planning and control to an emphasis on research, grantsmanship, and achievement

- To use bold and imaginative fund raising (in the original meaning of "development") as the principal lever for transforming the institution's image and reality
- To develop a more comprehensive budgeting/planning approach as a way of bringing coherence to a multiplicity of initiatives in a decentralized institution and to strengthen the institution financially.

The School of Veterinary Medicine. In his inaugural address, President Mayer expressed his belief that New England needed a School of Veterinary Medicine and suggested that Tufts University be the institution to develop one. New England had no veterinary school; indeed, it was more difficult for students from the region to get a veterinary education than to get into medical school. If the states in the region could provide some support for students and some capital and facilities, Tufts could organize the school. Apart from being attractive on its own merits, the program had a powerful leverage for Tufts. Adding a veterinary school would require the addition of a number of new basic science faculty members who could supplement the departments already serving the medical and dental schools, thereby enriching their mix enough to make the combined forces eligible for more-than-incremental grant support. Additional research possibilities also opened for collaboration among the clinical faculties.

President Mayer appointed a planning task force chaired by Thomas Murnane (then associate dean of the dental school and a person with extensive grantsmanship experience) and staffed by the author. While the charge to the task force was "to investigate the feasibility of starting a School of Veterinary Medicine," the group's real charge was to find a way to make it possible. Mayer and Murnane put together a combination of state-donated land and buildings, a federal start-up grant supported by the New England congressional delegation, and private financial support. The idea for the school—the strategic decision—was the president's. The task force contributed to the tactical planning, and a series of consultants, visiting committees, faculty groups, and administrators carried out the operational planning.

Nutrition. Nutrition was a natural for Mayer. His own teaching and research lay in this field. He had made major contributions to public education through widely syndicated newspaper columns and to the development of national nutrition programs through his chairmanship of the 1969 White House Conference on Food, Nutrition, and Health. Nutrition studies and research were relevant to the health science schools (including veterinary medicine) and, in their public policy dimensions, to programs of international development and domestic policy. The only nutrition-related programs in the region were those at the Harvard School of Public Health, then in substantial disarray and moving in new directions, and those at MIT (nutrition and food technology), also in disarray. If Tufts were going to move strongly in this area, however, it needed an anchor—a major research specialty of its own. Mayer found one in a congressionally authorized but unfunded U.S. Department of Agriculture (USDA) program for national nutrition research centers. He developed a program for a center focused on the relationship of nutrition and aging and was able to obtain federal funding for construction of a major facility to be operated by Tufts for the Department of Agriculture. The center receives substantial annual research support from USDA but also conducts related research for other federal agencies and corporations.

Here again, the strategic vision and the funding mechanisms were the president's. Mayer then brought to Tufts several faculty members from the Harvard and MIT programs. They, with Tufts' faculty and administrators, carried out the tactical and operational planning.

Environmental Management. Mayer undertook his nutrition and veterinary initiatives immediately. His third major programmatic thrust came several years later. The first two new programs were clear additions to Tufts: new programs, new facilities, new faculty, new funding. Both focused mainly on the health science activities on the Boston campus. It was a bit harder to find initiatives that would be as helpful on the liberal arts/engineering/graduate school campus. In particular, there was a desire to provide leverage for the College of Engineering. As Tufts' second biggest school, Engineering lacked centers of excellence that would give it distinctive strengths.

The solution was to undertake a major program in environmental management. National concern with environmental problems was rising. New and often multidisciplinary approaches were needed, and Tufts had relevant expertise in a number of areas, whereas no one else in New England had major programs in this field. The Environmental Protection Agency agreed to provide major initial and continuing grant support, and corporate contributions and involvement were sought to complement the federal funding. Unlike the nutrition and veterinary programs, which had their own dedicated faculty and facilities, the environmental initiative was conceived almost as a foundation—a device for developing and supporting key research initiatives in engineering, the related sciences, public policy departments, and the health sciences. The Center for Environmental Management outlined areas of principal programmatic interest and awarded its funds based on an internal competitive bidding process to faculty members or teams from such departments as Civil Engineering, Urban and Environmental Planning, Chemistry, and Public Health.

President Mayer and Vice-President Murnane (by now head of the development activity) developed the idea with help from several consultants. A director with extensive experience in the field was hired. He fleshed out the program with several additional new faculty-equivalent personnel and with Tufts faculty members and administrators.

Before going on to the other initiatives, it is worth noting that the three new programs had several elements in common:

- They were activities of intellectual and professional importance in their own right and would attract faculty Tufts could be proud of.
- No other university in the area had programs in these fields.
- They were activities of regional and national interest, programs that had political as well as intellectual support and could attract federal, foundation, and private funds.
- Each of them leveraged Tufts' internal resources by providing new faculty, new research possibilities, new facilities, and a bit of internal competition and stimulation to excel.

Entrepreneurial Liberation. The fourth initiative was very much Mayer's doing as well, though it took the form of a change in atmosphere rather than a specific program. Faculty members perceived it mainly as an acceleration into high gear of Wessell and Hallowell's emphasis on research competence when hiring new faculty and evaluating faculty performance. Administrators perceived it as an invitation to all kinds of new ideas and, sometimes, as an invitation to chaos. President Mayer was expecting everyone to play in the academic big leagues. That meant encouraging faculty members and deans to do what their equivalents at top research universities do—design their own programs, build their own teams, find their own support. If the old response to an idea was to ask the presenter to flesh it out and present it in the annual budget process, the response now was to wonder why the presenter was wasting time on approvals rather than taking it straight to a foundation or federal agency.

It is likely that this change in internal signals was partly a conscious strategy and partly a simple carryover of Mayer's training in the normal ways of functioning at major universities. In any event, the effect was gradual but profound. There has been a series of supportive tactical and operational planning endeavors designed to help the research effort grow: increasing the staffing in sponsored research offices, providing modest travel grants to faculty members to visit sponsoring agencies, providing seed money that faculty committees can award to promising faculty members, and asking deans to set targets for sponsored research. It may be symbolically important that the sponsored research officers reported to the development division until a few years ago. Today they report to the provost's office.

Deans were encouraged to be entrepreneurial for their own schools, and the decentralized nature of the university's budgeting system supported that initiative. Major programmatic changes and capital expenditures required administrative and board review, but if they were generally consistent with the mission of the school and with Mayer's level of aspiration for the university (and the schools could afford them), they were approved.

Fund Raising. President Mayer and Vice-President Murnane's intentional use of fund raising as the principal lever of change at Tufts may have been their single most important strategy. The incremental dollars were vital, to be sure. But even more important were the visibility and credibility Tufts acquired in the eyes of its internal and external constituencies by its ability to attract those new resources. In many ways, Tufts' development campaigns were, especially at the beginning, specifically planned for their leverage on institutional image.

As noted earlier, Tufts had had a singularly unimpressive fund-raising history. Unhappy with the fund-raising counsel's estimates of a yield of only $25 million for a capital campaign, Mayer sought new vision and leadership for the division. Murnane (whose background as an oral surgeon led to lots of comments about extractions) took on the challenge. He had no direct private fund-raising experience, but he did have extensive skills in grantsmanship and program development. Determined to succeed, willing to experiment, and willing to spend whatever it took to accomplish the mission, Murnane reconstituted the division. Campaigns were planned and carried out to provide support for both the new programmatic initiatives and the ongoing operations and to bring in dollars for programs, endowment, and buildings. They were conducted among traditional sources—alumni, foundations, friends, and the like—but also among individuals and organizations that had had no prior connection with Tufts but might be interested in the new activities. Finally, they sought support from both private and public sources. Mayer achieved early and highly visible successes in attracting federal support for the veterinary school, for the human nutrition research center, for an "intercultural center" headquarters for the Fletcher School, and later for a learning resources center for the health sciences. Murnane launched one of the first paid-student telethon efforts in the country, rapidly raising the percentage of alumni donors from less than 20 to almost 40 percent. An initial campaign goal of $140 million caused disbelief among some trustees and many administrators and faculty members, but it was met and surpassed within the planned time. A subsequent campaign for $250 million is now over halfway to completion and is also on schedule.

Credit for recognizing the need for vigorous fund raising and for having the confidence that Tufts could undertake it belong to Mayer. Credit for much of the strategic planning as well as for the tactical and operational planning goes to Murnane and his staff, with help from a variety of other administrators. (For more information on development planning, see the description of institution "Gamma" in Loessin and Duronio, in press.)

A Stronger Planning/Budgeting Process. Although the final strategic development was not directly a Mayer initiative, it was undertaken with his complete support. As the new ventures and the new spirit of enterprise began to take hold at Tufts, it was clear to the board that stronger budget management was needed. They had put a high-powered V-8 engine in the old car, and now had to improve the steering, the suspension, and perhaps the brakes.

The strategic decision was taken by key board members; tactical and operational planning was carried out over a number of years by senior administrative personnel. A new executive vice-president reorganized the administrative side of the house and began the process of building financial reserves. Frustrated with the excess of initiatives over resources, however, he stayed only one year. His successor, Steven S. Manos, accelerated the strengthening of Tufts' financial position and managed the planning/budgeting process so that it could function in a decentralized and increasingly entrepreneurial institution. Tufts had operated on an "every tub on its own bottom" philosophy for several years, but it concentrated on budgeting one year at a time.

Several steps were taken to transform this into a satisfactory planning/budgeting process. An overview of key planning assumptions, university priorities, and environmental conditions was developed and refined each year and was reviewed with the trustees as the first step in the annual cycle. Each dean was asked to present narrative goals and supporting statistics (such as faculty salaries, tuition rates, staffing patterns, and financial aid as percentages of tuition, both in historical perspective and compared with peer institutions) that supported his or her planned revenue and expenditure pattern. This policy allowed concentration on what was to be achieved, rather than on the details of the numbers. The planning horizon was extended to three years, rolling forward a year with each cycle. Capital budgets were added to operating budgets for a more comprehensive view of the financial management.

Tufts' Strategic Planning Process

The characterization of Tufts' planning process as entrepreneurial is accurate but incomplete. It is more than a series of brilliant responses to opportunities, though such responses have accounted for much of the university's impressive progress under Mayer's leadership. People at other universities often ask to see a copy of Tufts' strategic plan. In the sense of a single document that describes an overall plan and timetable, none exists. Those who know the institution often ask how priorities get set in this environment. Both questions deserve an answer, but the answers are not simple. Our plans and our priority setting emerge from a complex mix of managerial philosophies, a few overall guiding principles and priorities, an annual planning/budgeting process, and occasional opportunities for long-range thinking.

Philosophy. *Planning, decision making, authority, and responsibility must go together.* This sound managerial rule has several operational corollaries at Tufts. Tufts is managed on a decentralized basis. Major deans (Arts and Sciences, Medicine, and so forth) are held responsible for the full scope of leadership and management of their schools. Operationally, this every-tub-on-its-own-bottom approach means that planning and priority setting at Tufts consist largely of the planning by those deans for their schools. Most decisions are "compartmentalized." School plans and budgets are subject to review and approval by senior administration and the board. Unless overruled, however, each dean controls all major revenue decisions (how many students, what tuition to charge, and the like) and collects all revenues including endowment, gifts, and indirect cost reimbursement. Each is also responsible for all major expenditure decisions in that school (how many faculty, what to pay them, and so on) and must meet all direct and indirect costs. Any surpluses may be retained by the schools for use in subsequent years as approved by the board; any deficits must be repaid. This principle is overridden occasionally "to encourage or require schools to participate in programs or activities which they might otherwise choose to ignore, such as the all-University automated library system and the [new] Student Information System" (Manos, 1989, p. 2). In the absence of such an overriding priority, however, school deans and their faculties do the planning, make the decisions, and bear the consequences.

Strategic and tactical planning must be integrally linked with budgetary decision making and financial capital planning. We tend to avoid abstract university-wide wishful thinking and to concentrate on planning in the short, medium, and long term that provides a basis for specific decisions. For instance, a task force of academic and administrative managers has been working on providing a much-expanded set of facilities for engineering and the physical sciences. A second group has been developing plans for a similar expansion of research facilities for the Boston campus, working with real estate developers and R&D firms. A small working group has been developing plans for a major increase in the size and activities of the central library. Task forces on the two main campuses are planning major enhancements of the telecommunications and academic computing facilities. As these projects come to the point of decision, their conclusions are reflected in capital campaign plans, in construction schedules, and in operating budgets.

Significant changes happen only when outside conditions force them or someone inside decides to make them happen. If a college or university wants good management, it has to bring planning, decision making, responsibility, and authority together. It has to put people in charge with a major stake in the outcome of the process. If a school is going to progress, the dean has to make it progress. If a project is going to succeed, the project director's job has to depend on its succeeding. In each of Mayer's programmatic initiatives, an expert was brought into the university and given responsibility for making it work.

Overall Priorities and Principles. *Don't let the urgent override the important.* There are a few constant policies and principles that set boundaries on planning and decision making. Typically, these are articulated by the president and the board of trustees. Some are operating policies. The payout from endowment, for instance, will be 5 percent in current dollars above that of last year, regardless of market value, with 5 percent of the value of any new endowment gifts being added for the period of time they are held. Unrestricted bequests must be placed into endowment. Funding for plant renewal and adaptation (which was at a very low level) will be budgeted at steadily increasing levels by all schools. Other guidelines include the long-term goal of emphasizing scholarship and research among the faculty. Operationally, this goal not only involves standards for faculty appointment and promotion but includes the active seeking of opportunities for augmenting the space and support for research activities.

Occasional Overviews. *If you don't know where you want to go, any road will take you there.* Consistent with the view that planning makes no sense unless it is linked with decision making, we take advantage of opportunities to do somewhat longer-range integrative planning. In February 1987, the university launched the New Campaign for Tufts with a goal of $250 million. The targets for the campaign were based on an eighteen-month process that involved development of facility master plans for all four campuses, every dean's articulation of the needs of their school, and senior administration review of overall university priorities. President Mayer periodically articulates his sense of direction and goals for the university. He did so in his November 1985 annual report to the board of trustees, summarizing and basing his priorities on the results of a university-wide goal-setting process. Every few years the university reviews its capital and debt structure, particularly where new debt or refinancing may be needed. This review is also an opportunity for bringing together all the anticipated needs.

An Annual Planning/Budgeting Cycle. *At some point, plans and resources have to come together.* This mixture of entrepreneurial initiatives, operating philosophies, guiding principles, and occasional overviews would be unmanageable if we did not have an ongoing process that brings all these ideas together.

That process is a rolling three-year planning and budgeting cycle. Overall planning assumptions and major priorities are spelled out and reviewed at the start of the cycle. The school deans articulate plans for their schools in narrative form, highlighting assumptions about enrollments, student charges, compensation, faculty recruitment, curricula, facilities, and other critical factors. These plans are translated into both operating and capital budgets by the schools, spelling out the consequences of the proposed decisions over the three-year planning period. The university's central administration and the board of trustees review the planning assumptions and the budgets in detail before the board approves the student charges and major capital expenditures. This process provides "a discipline for decision-making and a boundary within which priorities must be established. . . . (Manos, 1989, p. 1). All projects, programs, and priorities are the subject of consensus building . . . as constituency politics comes into play. The development of a major addition to Cousens Gym is a perfect example of this, as the stated needs of the Athletics Department, the ability of our fund raisers to raise money for specific elements of the program, the views on needs of trustees and members of the board of overseers, and the overall guiding judgment of the president and his associates have influenced the decision-making" (Manos, 1989, p. 3).

Another helpful regular planning process involves a series of "rounds"— quarterly meetings at successively higher management levels at which facility priority decisions are established. Thus there is no overall "strategic plan" or priority-setting mechanism for Tufts University. There is instead a steadily evolving series of plans developed in response to presidential leadership and particular opportunities or needs. These plans shape the annual three-year planning and budgeting cycle and the concomitant capital financing plans but are, in turn, shaped by them.

Evaluation of This Approach

Like any other approach to planning and institutional change, the entrepreneurial style that has characterized Tufts over the last fourteen years has certain strengths and complementary weaknesses. Among the strengths are the following:

• The leading figures (President Mayer, Vice-President Murnane, and others) generate creative ideas that a constituency-based planning committee would be unlikely to produce. The important ideas are for changes in the institution, not refinements. They come from seeing possibilities in a larger context and from having a higher level of ambition for the institution. Constituency committees usually have a hard time visualizing and advocating significant changes.

• The person having the idea has a stake in realizing it. If that person is the president or someone else in a senior position, the chances are strong that he or she will find the ways and means to make the idea work. Ideas coming from a constituency committee may or may not find favor, and there is little the committee can do to follow up on an idea that is not favorably received.

• The senior officer (especially the president) who has the idea is in a position to make it succeed—to assign someone to make it happen and to make that person's job dependent on success. Often ideas proposed by a constituency committee just get added to an administrator's crowded job agenda and definition and do not spark the live-or-die attention they need to achieve success.

The weaknesses of this approach are the consequences of its strengths:

• The president cannot do everything. Some of the ideas may well fail simply because every human being has a finite level of attention and energy. To the extent that new ideas have no base of support and are not related to what is happening in the rest of the institution, they may not work.

• Chaos is always a possibility. Entrepreneurial leaders sometimes have more ideas than the institution can respond to and may favor their pet projects at the expense of other operations. New initiatives can overwhelm an orderly budgeting/planning process.

• The relationship among the new initiatives exists most clearly in the chief's head. Others may not see the connections and fail to take advantage of the intersections and overlapping implications.

• There can be a fair amount of wasted effort. After substantial time and funds have been expended on their development, some intriguing possibilities may turn out to be infeasible or to have undesirable consequences.

The entrepreneurial approach is an excellent vehicle for institutional change, but it may be disruptive when an institution really needs a refinement of its mission and character rather than a change. It is more likely to fit in a private institution than a public one, given the former's higher degree of local autonomy. It needs to be supplemented by second-level administrators with both a dedication to delivering on the changes and the skills to manage an ongoing operation in the process. Above all, the entrepreneurial process stands or falls on the ability of the president and his or her senior colleagues to perceive unmet needs, to find ways to use them to leverage the institution, to assess the risks and investments astutely, and to lead the faculty, key administrators, and staff through the change process.

Role of Institutional Research

An institutional research and planning office can play an indispensable role in support of formal planning processes, especially those that involve constituency-based committees for which the office provides informational and logistical support. My first job at Tufts was to staff a university-wide long-range planning effort of just this sort. Finding the most effective ways to support an entrepreneurial planning approach involved some trial and error. On two or three occasions, responding to requests from other senior administrators or the board of trustees, I attempted to start up committee-based comprehensive planning efforts. They were largely a waste of time, since they often were unrelated to specific decisions that needed to be made and tended to have only token attention from those who were really moving the institution forward.

On the other hand, working on specific projects was highly productive. The key was to identify the person (usually a dean or operating vice-president) responsible for making something happen and to find ways to help that person deliver. The office could make real contributions to the group that was planning the veterinary school, to those making major curricular changes in the dental school, to the deans and the development planners working out the goals for the capital campaign, to the environmental management center planners, and to those working on many other initiatives and projects.

A major contribution of a more systematic nature was the joint effort of the planning and budgeting offices in developing the rolling three-year planning/budgeting process. If we were to do without overall comprehensive planning (and it was clear that such planning was likely to be counterproductive), then at least the planning office could help design a process in which all the relevant information and decisions came together.

All of these efforts, both the new initiatives and the ongoing operational planning for the university, required information support. A comprehensive *Fact Book* brought together information on the university. Innumerable comparative studies measured one or another aspect of the university's operations against similar activities elsewhere so that we could understand our status, our opportunities, and our progress.

The basic principles for planning in this environment, and possibly in others, seem clear: Get to know the values, history, and relevant dimensions of the institution. Get to know those who really make a difference and find out what they want to accomplish. Then find ways to help them evaluate the feasibility of their dreams and ways to help them make the dreams come true.

References

Loessin, B. A., and Duronio, M. A. "The Role of Planning in Successful Fund-Raising in Ten Higher Education Institutions." *Planning for Higher Education*, forthcoming.

Manos, S. S. "University and School Priorities." Unpublished memo to the Administration and Finance Committee of the Trustees of Tufts College, July 12, 1989.

John A. Dunn, Jr., is executive director of the Center for Planning Information at Tufts University. He was at Tufts from 1969 through 1989, the last eight years as vice-president for planning. He is currently president of the Society for College and University Planning.

Creative planning transformed an old and troubled institution into a success story.

Planning at a Small Institution: Bradford College

Janice S. Green

The story of Bradford College from 1981 to the present is one of transformation and revitalization. It is the story of a deeply troubled small liberal arts college that, in spite of fiscal constraints, has progressed to where it is described by others as a pathfinder in higher education.

This chapter describes the decision making and planning that shaped Bradford's progress. Fundamental to the college's advancement have been strong and creative leadership, planning focused on institutional mission and purpose, maintaining a healthy tension between consensus building and the need to move ahead boldly, and a measure of carefully considered risk taking. As a key figure in the Bradford story, this writer cannot claim total lack of bias. In retrospect, however, it is plain that errors were made even as successes accumulated. Perhaps in crisis situations this is inevitable. Nonetheless, describing the steps taken to produce the Bradford turnaround may help similar institutions struggling to survive in difficult times.

The Setting

Bradford College is a private, coeducational, four-year liberal arts college located 35 miles north of Boston. Eighty-five percent of its 450 students are residential and, although predominantly drawn from the northeast, the population includes substantial representation from western and midwestern states and from abroad.

Bradford opened its doors in 1803 as an academy for local boys and girls. In the course of its long history it evolved first into a secondary school for girls, gradually added a postsecondary curriculum, and in 1932

NEW DIRECTIONS FOR INSTITUTIONAL RESEARCH, no. 67, Fall 1990 © Jossey-Bass Inc., Publishers

became Bradford Junior College for Women, offering a two-year program in the liberal arts and sending its graduates on to selective institutions nationwide. It was one of the "Three B's," Bennett, Briarcliff, and Bradford. By the late 1960s, however, it was clear that the heyday of the junior college for women was over. Bennett and Briarcliff would soon close. Bradford opted to respond yet again to social change, becoming in 1971 a coeducational college offering the bachelor of arts degree. Only later did the trustees, administration, and faculty begin to discover the complexities of their undertaking. Ten years later, Bradford was still "in transition," a euphemism for chronic loss of direction and purpose.

Those responsible in 1971 had failed to recognize a central truth: Switching gears to coeducation and baccalaureate instruction entails a great deal more than adding some upper-level courses, packaging a few majors, and assigning dormitory rooms to male students. The single-sex junior college is characterized by a particular campus culture and set of traditions. Moreover, its organizational structure, curriculum, faculty, and policies and procedures generally are inappropriate to the mission of a senior institution. Few of these issues had been addressed. And so, despite the obvious commitment of trustees, faculty, and staff, Bradford College was adrift. It remained in essence a two-year college offering the bachelor's degree to the small number of students who chose to remain for four years.

By the fall of 1981, the college suffered from a number of potentially fatal illnesses: loss of institutional identity, fiscal distress, declining enrollment, a seriously unhappy and powerless faculty, dwindling standards, and a poorly defined curriculum. The incumbent president, a trustee and alumna, had been appointed two years earlier to keep the college afloat through her skills as professional fund raiser. Having succeeded at this seemingly impossible task, she would shortly announce her resignation. Meanwhile, an emergency plan for closing the college had been developed by the trustees—just in case.

First Steps to Revitalization

In 1981–82 it was clear to the campus newcomer—myself—that setting new directions for Bradford would be next to impossible unless a number of preliminary steps were taken. Most critical was the need to restore the confidence of the faculty and return to them an appropriate role in institutional governance, a role almost totally eroded during a two-year period of top-down administration. Actions were needed to heal the painful wounds inflicted by inexperienced leadership that truly did not understand the dynamics and traditions of academe, lessen the anxiety about whether the college would close down, and revise faculty personnel policies and procedures that had remained unchanged since the days of Bradford Junior College. All these concerns had resulted, a year earlier, in a faculty effort to unionize. This initiative was blocked by the board of trustees who brought the case to the National Labor Relations Board (NLRB), citing the Yeshiva decision. Since Bradford's case was still pending, it was essential to move quickly.

At midyear we learned of the NLRB ruling. The Bradford faculty did have the right to unionize. A vote must be taken within ninety days. By the date of the vote taking, much had been accomplished. Bradford's first faculty rank and promotion system was established, along with formal criteria and procedures for faculty evaluation. Multiple-year faculty contracts were initiated. Support for faculty development was increased. Revision of an outdated and confusing faculty manual had begun. Most significant, a legitimate system of faculty governance was restored. Each step, even though requiring subsequent refinement, moved the faculty toward an enhanced self-image and a renewed sense of optimism. When the vote was taken that spring, unionization was rejected.

The reader may be wondering how all of this could have transpired so quickly. Two factors contributed: first, the commitment of the faculty to the college despite their aggrieved condition and, second, the fact that the new academic dean acted much more boldly than would be the case in the future. Fully developed proposals introducing new policies were presented in rapid succession to an elected group, the Faculty Affairs Committee. Discussions were held and minor revisions introduced. Recommendations were brought by the committee to the full faculty, approved, and implemented. By the following year faculty were ranked, a Promotion Committee elected, and formal faculty contracts (yet another innovation) issued.

A second focus of my attention in 1981–82 was the curriculum. Whatever new initiatives lay in the future, they would have to be preceded by what was essentially a cleanup operation. A cursory study revealed poorly subscribed majors and duplicative courses, neither of which the college could afford. Working through the Curriculum Committee, traditionally chaired at Bradford by the academic dean, the academic divisions were asked to screen all courses listed in the catalogue, eliminate those not taught in the past three years, and delete or consolidate courses with duplicative content as well as those that did not contribute specifically to current program objectives. This effort led to a proposal by the dean to reduce the number of majors, all interdisciplinary, from seven to four. The changes involved nothing more than a repackaging of courses to create stronger programs. Since faculty positions were not jeopardized, the proposal was quickly approved.

In summary, that first year of Bradford's renewal was a time of laying the groundwork for the real planning efforts soon to begin. It was a task similar to that of preparing the soil before designing and planting a garden—a lot of digging and raking and generally cleaning up the landscape. If the head gardener assumed a more energetic, proactive role than is generally deemed acceptable among faculties, it was because the situation called for strong leadership and immediately visible progress. It was a gamble and it worked. Had the faculty voted to unionize, the trustees would have closed the college. Instead, the campus community began to feel a measure of hope and satisfaction from seeing that positive change was possible.

There are two lessons to be gleaned here. In a crisis situation, a measure of risk taking is probably unavoidable. However, the needs and purposes underlying the gamble must be clearly understood and endorsed by those involved. In this instance, the faculty's unhappiness and insecurity were so pervasive that the measures proposed were seen by the majority as positive steps toward improving their condition. Those few who preferred to maintain the status quo would choose, or be encouraged, to leave during the ensuing years.

The second lesson bears on the need to prepare for a major planning effort, particularly at a small institution. Planning for the future will have a greater potential for success if care is taken to at least begin to alleviate existing tensions or problems. If a generally positive attitude can be cultivated, there will be a willingness to take the next and often more difficult steps in a consensual mode. While it would be an exaggeration to claim that the work of 1981–82 brought a glowing sense of accomplishment to the campus, it did create a forward-looking, optimistic environment in which to plant the seeds of the future. We were as ready as we could be for the next steps.

Roots of the Transformation

After an intensive national search, the fall semester of 1982 saw the arrival of a new president, Dr. Arthur Levine. President Levine brought with him unquenchable energy, a profound understanding of higher education, and a vision on which to build Bradford's future. He was, admittedly, seeking a laboratory to test out hypotheses and findings developed over years of research and consultation in American colleges and universities. Given the concept he would present, Bradford was an exceptionally suitable site because it was small, by long tradition dedicated to the liberal arts and to interdisciplinarity, and by virtue of its fiscal problems, ripe for change. The college, for its part, sought strong, creative leadership and new directions. It was an ideal marriage.

The vision offered by Levine and described in broad strokes even during the interview stage of the search was ideal for Bradford. It would become known as "The Bradford Plan for a Practical Liberal Arts Education." The Bradford Plan is a comprehensive, cohesive, four-year program of studies encompassing both the curriculum and the co-curriculum and grounded in certain basic assumptions. It assumes, for example, that the best undergraduate education will prove useful to the student over a lifetime. It assumes also that a liberal arts education offers the broadest, richest, and most durable utility. It further assumes that men and women, like it or not, will spend forty or fifty years working, whether at a job, as citizens, or as family members. And, finally, it assumes that the kinds of work people do, and the demands placed upon them, will change frequently over the years.

The program that emerged from the original concept has been fully described elsewhere (Ranslow and Haselkorn, 1985; Gilley, Fulmer, and Reithling Shoefer, 1986). Most important from the perspective of this chapter is to understand that the Bradford Plan is more than a program of studies. It is nothing less than the actualization of Bradford's mission and thus clearly the motivating force behind all planning initiatives. Imagine the spokes of a wheel extending outward from the hub, and you will visualize planning at Bradford as it emanates directly from a central mission and set of purposes manifested in the Bradford Plan.

The essential goal of planning, therefore, is to support and enhance that mission. This is particularly significant because a small college cannot reproduce the breadth and depth of educational options offered at a larger institution. Rather, we must define what we can do better than, or differently from, the larger institution and focus planning activities on developing distinctive qualities and characteristics. In Bradford's case uniqueness was translated into a comprehensive approach to preparing students for life and work through the study of the liberal arts and sciences, providing diverse and increasingly challenging opportunities for applying knowledge and skills, and building upon such strengths as interdisciplinarity, emphasis on teaching effectiveness, and an interactive campus community.

The Work Begins

In September 1982, President Levine sent a proposal to the Curriculum Committee outlining in conceptual and organizational terms his vision of the Bradford Plan. This concept had already been introduced during the search process. By mid-October the proposal had been fully discussed and approved by the committee, endorsed by the full faculty, and shortly thereafter accepted by the board of trustees. The speed of the approval process was a clear signal of institutional readiness and desire for change. Now the much more difficult task of translating concept into programmatic reality would begin.

The Curriculum Committee was charged by the president with the task of program development. A timetable was prepared by the dean and accepted by the committee. It called for three years of curriculum development, phased implementation, and ongoing evaluation. Target dates for completion of curricular segments were based on the publication schedule for the annual college catalogue. If new courses were to appear in the following year's catalogue, they would require faculty approval by a specific date each spring. This device provided an impersonal but effective spur for maintaining momentum and progress. If all went according to schedule, the Bradford Plan would be fully in place at the end of three years.

The Curriculum Committee met weekly for two years. Individual faculty members were asked to take responsibility for the design and initial teaching of each of the general education core courses—a 24-credit required sequence broadly described in the Levine proposal. Faculty, in turn, consulted with their colleagues individually and in informal group discussions. Draft course descriptions and syllabi were brought to the committee, studied, and returned for revision, often several times. Subcommittees focused on other tasks—for example, the development of an internship program. Each course and curricular segment, once approved in committee, came to the full faculty for debate and action. Faculty workshops were held twice each year to consider specific elements of the new curriculum.

Two unrelated but perhaps predictable problems made that first year of program development extremely difficult. First, the administration never had anticipated the speed of faculty and board action in endorsing the Bradford Plan. At least a semester of debate had been expected, time badly needed to seek outside funding support. Second, an extremely tight budget did not permit release time for faculty engaged in developing the new curriculum. With a standard teaching load of 12 credits each semester, the burden was heavy. Despite the pervasive goodwill and enthusiasm, it was clear that the pace would be difficult to maintain. Surfacing as well was the realization that program development must be accompanied by faculty development. Bradford needed help.

In the late spring of 1983, good news arrived from the Fund for the Improvement of Postsecondary Education (FIPSE). Bradford was awarded a two-year grant of $56,000 to support the development of its new curriculum. It was the first grant of any consequence the college had ever received. The FIPSE grant was significant in several respects: It provided needed funds for faculty release time, consultants, and travel to conferences; it put a stamp of approval on a groundbreaking venture; it boosted confidence and morale; and it unlocked the doors of other major foundations. If FIPSE was interested in a small, little-known college, other groups were willing to take a look. They did just that, and in the ensuing years Bradford received generous support from many major foundations. It is not easy for colleges like Bradford to break into the world of foundations accustomed to funding a handful of favored institutions. It is, however, not only possible but necessary; planners are well advised to fold the issue of grantsmanship into their activities.

With the injection of new funds, the stages of program development proceeded on schedule. Consultant specialists came and went, bringing valuable insights and criticism. New core courses were offered—first as electives (the "dry run" period) and subsequently revised. Senior seminars took shape. Recruitment literature was rewritten to reflect Bradford's metamorphosis.

One area, however, became a center of controversy. The Levine proposal included a mandatory internship in the junior year. Faculty, however, were divided over the merits of the internship. Many believed that learning should take place in the classroom, laboratory, or studio. Some feared erosion of numbers in upper-level courses and weakening of the curriculum. Given the lack of consensus, the internship was designated an elective program. It was not a time for confrontation. There are moments when it is necessary to "go to the mat" and other moments when it is preferable to let matters evolve toward desired ends. The latter has proved to be the case. Today the internship is required in one of five majors and, at the request of faculty, is cited in the catalogue as "strongly recommended for all students." More than two-thirds of our graduates of the past three years have completed an internship and the number is growing. Others take a semester of study abroad as an alternative. The desired ends have been accomplished without threatening faculty prerogatives or a collegial environment.

Next Steps

Central to curricular planning were mechanisms for ongoing evaluation. It was universally recognized that continuous scrutiny of both the parts and the whole would be the only means of ensuring the validity of directions and the quality of results. Evaluation began with the assistance of consultants invited to review segments of the core curriculum once they had been offered on a trial basis. Students were asked to evaluate individual courses by completing an instrument designed to determine not only their reaction to courses but their understanding of course objectives. Each step of evaluation led to revision and refinement of courses.

Three years after full implementation, a faculty task force was established by the president and asked to spend a year in a comprehensive review of the Bradford Plan. Their work included interviews with faculty and students, examination of syllabi, class visitations, analysis of previous evaluation data, small group discussions, and much more. The resultant report was invaluable both in reaffirming a strong commitment to the program and in offering a series of recommendations for improvement. Most of those recommendations have since been implemented.

The following year a second faculty task force was charged to review the comprehensive major, the only element of the Bradford Plan in place prior to 1982. This review was occasioned by mounting evidence that the academic divisions had begun to tinker with their majors in order to provide a better fit with the core curriculum and the required senior project. Although well intended, these initiatives were creating a discomforting loss of focus and consistency. After six months of study, the task force presented a cogent definition of the Bradford major, its purposes and objectives, and recommendations calling for a common curricular structure and set of policies to be adopted by each division. Today, two years later, each Bradford major has been revised by divisional faculty in line with the recommendations of the task force.

A significant step was taken in 1987 with the appointment of a faculty member as general education core coordinator. Interestingly, the recommendation to appoint a coordinator had come several years earlier from a consultant. Strong opposition from the faculty at that time laid that recommendation to rest. Later, however, faculty recognized the need for better coordination and integration of core courses and for leadership directed specifically toward enhancing a critically important element of the Bradford Plan. This change of heart might be termed yet another example of the dictum "evolution is preferable to revolution." It also was evidence of the faculty's growing professionalism and ability to recognize and address programmatic needs.

Yet another advance was achieved in the sciences, virtually moribund after years of neglect by previous administrations. In 1984, the academic dean appointed a small faculty committee to consider the future of the sciences at Bradford. Although that group did not produce a particularly helpful document, it did offer public support for the establishment of an interdisciplinary major in the natural sciences and mathematics. Major funding was subsequently obtained from two foundations for renovating and re-equipping Bradford's science facilities, additional science faculty were appointed, a new academic division was created, and a program developed that is beginning to attract numbers of students. Plans for increasing these numbers involve the admissions and public relations offices and the efforts of the science faculty who are assisting regional public schools with their programs and, not incidentally, implanting an awareness of Bradford as a good place to come for students interested in science.

One further aspect of building the Bradford Plan is important to mention. Both the administration and faculty leadership recognized the need for developmental activities designed to strengthen the curriculum and support professional growth among the faculty. This need has been addressed in two ways. Seminars are offered each summer to groups of ten faculty focused primarily on the theories and pedagogies of critical thinking and writing across the curriculum, cornerstones of the Bradford Plan. The seminars have been funded by foundation grants. By now each faculty member has participated in at least one seminar. In addition, faculty have been funded to attend seminars offered by the University of Chicago and Bard College, and distinguished specialists are brought to campus to share their expertise. These programs are developed jointly by administration and faculty.

The professional needs of individual faculty are supported by the operating budget of the college through a fund controlled and dispersed by the Faculty Affairs Committee. Although the fund is not as large as we would like, it assists faculty with such activities as research projects, travel to conferences, and preparing exhibits and publications. While teaching effectiveness is the primary criterion for retention and promotion at Bradford, some evidence of professional development, broadly defined, is expected. Indeed, the results of the strategies described here have been truly amazing. Despite heavy workloads, faculty productivity in terms of publication and presentation of papers, exhibits, and concerts, to say nothing of new course preparation, is of excellent quality and ever-increasing quantity. Planning for the future most certainly will include the need to seek increased support for all modes of faculty development. This is ultimately the most cost-effective means of ensuring a vibrant and dynamic faculty.

This is not the place to describe the myriad refinements of the Bradford Plan since its inception. More germane is a consideration of the kinds of planning that occurred, shifts in planning strategies, and means of goal setting. Admittedly, those in leadership roles in the early 1980s were not what might be termed "systems people." Nor did they have the time or resources to prepare a comprehensive planning document. Time was critical. It was essential to demonstrate, and demonstrate quickly, that Bradford was on the move in directions that would restore three elements: a sense of purpose, a sense of institutional identity, and a sense of optimism. The urgency of the moment demanded strong leadership, setting decisive deadlines, and placing heavy burdens on staff and faculty. In the best of worlds, we would have moved at a pace more conducive to reflection and study of each proposal. A slower pace would have resulted in a better initial product and greatly reduced the need for subsequent rethinking and revision. That, however, was a luxury the college could ill afford. Perhaps the key ingredient to be weighed by institutions in similar situations is the desire of those immediately concerned—trustees, faculty, staff, and students—for change. If that desire is strong and widespread, risk taking can be successful. If not, plans are likely to backfire.

By 1985-86, the Bradford Plan was fully in place and the pace deliberately slowed to a less intense level. It was time for the administration to assume a more low-key position and promote faculty ownership of the Bradford Plan—in short, to serve primarily as resource and sounding board for the ideas that were flourishing among the faculty. Indeed, the vital energy aroused by the work of the past years had stimulated a flow of ideas. The academic divisions and faculty committees developed plans for further enrichment of the curriculum and took them through established approval procedures. Everyone, it appeared, was thinking in terms of setting goals, raising standards, and establishing programmatic objectives.

At this point, it may appear to the reader that Bradford has been in a continual state of ferment. To some extent this is true. The ferment signifies that the climate in which planning takes place at Bradford not only allows for change but assumes the inevitability of change. It is understood on campus that each generation of students (a period of about five years) not only faces new societal demands, but enters college equipped somewhat differently from its predecessors. Therefore, planning for change is unavoidable, as is the necessity to be ever alert for signs of new or different needs. At Bradford, there is an ongoing effort to inform faculty and staff of warning signals derived from institutional data and alert them to events and trends in the world "outside the gates" that call for a response. Intelligent response is a habit that can be formed. Another major factor in stimulating ideas and change is institutional size and organization. The thirty-five full-time faculty are organized in five multidisciplinary divisions. Not only are divisional members constantly in contact with one another, but faculty across divisions talk and plan together. Often faculty from different divisions will team teach. Committee structures promote debate. In a common dining room, faculty, staff, and students lunch together and exchange ideas. Senior administrators are readily accessible. A small college that does not take advantage of the opportunities afforded by size or tries to replicate the organizational and political patterns of the university is giving up an enormous advantage. Planning, we have learned, need not be confined to the boardroom.

Noncurricular Planning

The preceding pages have described a process of curriculum reform and implementation. Other areas of institutional planning for the past eight years have focused on three issues: developing the fiscal and human resources needed to support the Bradford Plan, establishing a recognizable new identity for the college externally as well as internally, and expanding the Bradford Plan to include the co-curriculum. Two years ago a fourth issue was added to the agenda: planning for growth.

The issue of institutional identity was linked to successful admission results and to fund raising. Ways had to be found to inform and convince the various publics that Bradford College was a four-year coeducational institution offering a unique curriculum—one linked to the traditions of the past but transformed in exciting ways to serve the present and future. A first symbolic step, ordered by the president, was to eliminate all physical evidence on campus of past identity as Bradford Junior College. The "Junior" on Bradford chairs was painted out. Bradford Junior College bookplates were replaced. The Alumnae Room became the Alumni Room, and Alumnae House underwent a similar name change. These were small but visible signs of a new era.

But the much larger task of establishing recognition as a baccalaureate institution among external groups—prospective students and parents, guidance counselors, alumni, the local community—would prove to be far more difficult. We discovered that memories die hard. Many hours were spent by the president and his cabinet in seeking affordable ways to communicate a new image. Consultants assisted with market surveys and redesign of college literature. The admissions staff was expanded modestly to permit increased visits to high schools and college fairs across the country. Presentations were made at major professional conferences, and the Ford Foundation sponsored a high-level conference at Bradford on the value of the liberal arts. Opportunities were created to attract the attention of local and national media. We discovered, interestingly, that it is much easier to get the message across to educators and to the media than to local residents. Even now, almost twenty years after Bradford's shift to coeducation and baccalaureate status, neighbors are apt to refer to the college as BJC and wonder when we began admitting males.

For many of the older alumnae, the changes have been particularly difficult to accept. They remember a pristine campus where young ladies wore white blazers, entertained male friends in a formal reception room, and attended chapel regularly. The alumni of the 1970s, on the other hand, harbor negative feelings about the college—"the bad old days"—and are not eager to be supportive. The task of kindling renewed enthusiasm in the alumni body continues to challenge the administration. The president and others, including faculty and students, crisscross the country speaking to alumni groups. Reunion weekends feature the new curriculum as a natural outgrowth of the past. Alumni publications nostalgically recall the old while highlighting today's progress. Although the process will take time, progressive increases in the amount and participation rate of annual giving show that the message is taking hold.

In 1984, planning began for the college's first capital campaign. The goal was $5 million earmarked for the endowment with a completion date of three years. Consultants were hired to assist a small development staff. Planning for the campaign was the responsibility of the president, the vice-president for college relations, and the development committee of the board of trustees. Formally announced one year later, the goal was reached six months ahead of schedule. While the campaign was successful, an important lesson was learned. An enormous burden of travel and solicitation was assumed by too few people, the president and a handful of trustees. The next campaign, projected to begin within a few years, is much more ambitious and will benefit from the earlier experience. Already campaign staffing has increased significantly, research is well under way, and cultivation of prospects has begun. Most important, perhaps, trustees and alumni networks are being educated to the role they will have to assume during the next campaign.

A critical issue during the mid 1980s was the low level of faculty and staff salaries. It was an issue causing widespread dissatisfaction and the departure of valuable people. The administration and trustees decided to address the question of faculty salaries first; resources did not permit campus-wide increases. The academic and fiscal vice-presidents worked for a year with the Faculty Affairs Committee to devise a three-year program of salary improvement that would not only raise salaries to a level commensurate with comparable institutions, but would eliminate inequities among salaries within ranks. Salary data were collected for thirteen comparable institutions.

The planning process was open, collegial, and realistic. During each of the program years, the group met to review, adjust figures, and assess progress. Since the successful conclusion of the program the salary schedule has been scrutinized and refined annually by administrators and faculty representatives working together. The process worked because budget information was freely shared and guidelines developed consensually. It produced a great deal of goodwill and a marked reduction in faculty departures. Institutions that embark on a similar program should recognize, however, that it calls for patience, a willingness to listen, and at least one able negotiator. Moreover, if it is not possible to improve salaries campus-wide, expressions of dissatisfaction should be expected from the groups who must wait. Despite reassurances of things to come, this occurred at Bradford. And though staff and administrative salaries and benefits were eventually improved quite substantially, the scars remain. In retrospect this is a classic case of decision making resulting in a trade-off: the improvement of one situation to the detriment of another. Planners are well advised to weigh carefully the pluses and minuses of any trade-off.

Another major planning issue of the mid 1980s stemmed from the wish to develop a co-curriculum that reflected the educational objectives of the curriculum. We believe that the co-curriculum, or life outside the classroom, should be part and parcel of a total learning experience. Accordingly, student activities and residence life programs should reflect such purposes as the development of leadership, responsibility, independence, and creativity. The vice-president for student affairs was charged by the president with preparing that route. The process began at the cabinet level when the president and senior officers spent many hours compiling a list of the attributes and characteristics, both intellectual and personal, that a Bradford education should nurture. That list was presented by the vice-president for student affairs to his staff for study and refinement. Student development specialists came to campus to work with staff. Several key policy decisions resulted.

It was determined, for example, that student activities, in order to meet student interests while fostering leadership and related skills, should be initiated by students, not staff. If a student or group wishes to promote a club, community service project, or event, support is available. Club sports are also initiated by students. As student interest dies, so does the activity. The results have been extremely positive. Students who remain uninvolved are in the minority and the campus bustles with varied activity. Shifting from top-down planning to a student-centered approach cannot happen overnight, however. In fact, it may require several years. Recently I overheard a freshman tell a prospective student that "at Bradford you can make anything happen if you set your mind to it."

Essentially the same approach was applied to residential life and student governance. Plans were developed by the student affairs staff for improved training of resident assistants, preliminary to gradually shifting the responsibility for monitoring the residence halls from professional to student staff. Now, after three years, each dormitory is staffed by a student head resident and a group of assistants. Professional staff no longer live in the dorms.

Similarly, the former College Council, composed of students, faculty, and staff, has given way to an elected student government responsible for the allocation and disbursement of student activity funds and other tasks. These changes implement policies and plans established to further the educational purposes of the college. Do things always run smoothly? Of course not. Are the wrinkles still being ironed out? Absolutely. Nevertheless, students, faculty, and staff alike are pleased with the knowledge that Bradford endorses a holistic mode of education and is willing to take a few risks.

More recently planning for the co-curriculum has involved the development of a co-curricular transcript for each student. This document will record student activities, accomplishments, and on-campus and off-campus jobs in terms of acquired skills and personal characteristics—the same list of educational goals that was devised several years ago. It will be used by students and advisers for planning and guidance and can be presented to prospective employers and graduate schools as evidence of accomplishment. Involved in this new venture are student development and career counseling staff, faculty, the registrar, and a number of students. The process serves as an example of diverse offices working together on an experimental project that mirrors the interdisciplinary nature of the curriculum. In broader terms it may be seen as a model for small-scale planning that brings together unrelated groups, fosters communication and understanding, and nurtures fundamental institutional objectives.

Planning for the Future

One central issue has triggered a major new phase of planning. That issue is growth. The student population has increased by almost 25 percent in the past several years. The full-time faculty now numbers thirty-five, up from twenty-five in 1981–82. Professional and support staffs have grown proportionately. Each aspect of growth has raised large questions. What is the optimum size for the student body? What will additional numbers of students require in terms of new faculty and staff? Should the focus be on building the endowment or on bricks and mortar? Can salaries keep pace with those at comparable institutions? In view of the declining numbers of traditional-age college students, should emphasis be placed on strengthening student recruitment or retention or both?

In the summer of 1988, the trustees met in retreat with the senior officers. A long-range planning committee was appointed and charged with the task of preparing short-term and long-term plans for the future of the college. Two central issues quickly emerged. The first was that of size. Earlier studies had shown that although there are precious benefits to be gained from being a very small institution, there are also significant disadvantages. Economies of scale are impossible. A study by Cambridge Associates had shown that growth was essential to the long-term fiscal health of the college. The student perspective on size, obtained through surveys and exit interviews, was particularly revealing. While students universally appreciated the opportunity for extensive interaction with faculty, small classes, and the chance to be a big fish in a small pond, many also experienced the loss of privacy that occurs when the pond comes to resemble a goldfish bowl. Some students described a sense of claustrophobia; many others believed that bigger is better. For faculty, Bradford's present size means insufficient contact with colleagues in their own discipline. It became clear that continued growth was vital. The planners concluded that a student body of 650 to 700 would preserve Bradford's special qualities while addressing student and faculty concerns and strengthening the college's fiscal position. It was agreed that growth should be incremental and directed toward increasing selectivity.

The second major issue was that of physical plant. Bradford sits on a remarkably beautiful 75-acre campus. Its buildings, however, were designed for a smaller and much different institution. The newest buildings date back to the early 1960s. And despite recent investment, the neglect of the fiscally troubled years resulted in a condition politely termed "tattered elegance." In short, the place was shabby and could not support Bradford's programs. Both restoration and expansion were needed. To cite one glaring example, the building that houses our undersized gymnasium, circa 1904, has been declared a historical monument. Prospective students seem largely unimpressed by that fact. Planning for growth demanded planning for facilities as well.

The services of a consulting firm were enlisted to study needs and develop a campus design for the future. Concurrently college staff analyzed data to determine, for example, personnel needs to support growth, endowment increase required to support higher operating costs, implications for fund raising, scheduling the construction of a new dormitory, and much more. As the list of needs grew, it became clear that setting priorities was necessary. If Bradford was to attract and retain larger numbers of well-qualified students, should the first priority be refurbishment, library expansion, a new field house, or a new student center/dining complex? All were needed and all depended on acquiring a large number of dollars.

At this point, two significant events occurred. First, President Levine announced his impending resignation to assume the directorship of the Harvard University Institute of Educational Management. Second, the trustees opted to raise $5 million as an enrichment fund for refurbishment, preparing for a major capital campaign, salary enhancement, and three new faculty positions. This proved to be a wise decision. Most of the $5 million has been raised, the new faculty are in place, campaign planning is under way, and staff salaries have been upgraded. New furnishings, carpeting, and paint are restoring Bradford's attractiveness.

In July 1989, Dr. Joseph Short assumed the presidency of Bradford College. He has brought us needed strengths and experience in fiscal management, fund raising, and planning for nonprofit organizations. Since his arrival, emphasis has been placed on setting goals for the future, financial planning, and enrollment management. A second long-range planning committee will soon be appointed to update and refine the original planning document. This committee, unlike the first, will include full participation by faculty members. That oversight was a serious mistake not to be repeated. The new planning group will benefit from much more sophisticated financial and development data than was previously available, thanks to computer systems installed three years ago and only now beginning to realize their full value. Other information systems are still in a fairly elementary stage and are slated for upgrading. Nevertheless, planners at small institutions should be encouraged to move ahead even lacking state-of-the-art resources. Pencils and calculators produce results, too, albeit more slowly.

Thanks to President Short's extensive involvement with international development and education, efforts have begun to strengthen the Bradford Plan's focus on the world as a global community. A multifaceted program designed to encourage retention is in preparation. Publications will take on a new look. And the development staff is putting in long hours preparing for a major fund-raising effort.

Lessons Learned

A basic principle of the Bradford Plan is that the best way to learn is by doing. In reviewing the events of the past eight years, it appears that the same principle applies to planning. Levine brought to Bradford a concept of liberal arts education. That concept became reality through a process of planned development, implementation, and assessment. Short has brought a concept upon which to base institutional growth and advancement. Many now are involved in implementing that concept. The central lesson is that planning emanating directly from a sharply defined institutional mission and set of purposes will be most successful. The path must be defined before planning can begin. Even if the planners occasionally stray, they will soon realize their mistake and retrace their steps. Indeed, they will become more surefooted as they advance.

Bradford's revitalization was possible largely because of the qualities of leadership, the rare devotion and commitment of so many, and the confidence that prevailed even in thorny moments. Planning itself cannot account for these wonderful assets. Planning can only channel movement toward the future. Perhaps it is largely the result of a happy marriage of mission and planning that Bradford has come to be recognized as a success story. Even more basic, however, is the solid consensus relative to mission and implementation that Bradford has enjoyed. That is the real secret of success. "Know thyself" is a message that applies equally to individuals and to institutions. Recognition of strengths and weaknesses, identification of values and aspirations—these are the signs of readiness to move ahead. Planning is merely the tool for realizing goals: its form will vary according to the institution. As Bradford has changed, so too has its planning changed, moving toward more and more formalized structures. This is neither good nor bad. It means simply that, like curricula, planning mechanisms must evolve and mature in order to remain vital. Today Bradford's future looks bright. Intelligent, creative planning will help to ensure that brightness does not dim.

References

Gilley, J. W., Fulmer, K. A., and Reithling Shoefer, S. J. Searching for Academic Excellence: Twenty Colleges and Universities on the Move and Their Leaders. New York: Macmillan, 1986.
Ranslow, P., and Haselkorn, D. "Bradford College: Curriculum Reform and Institutional Renewal." In J. Green, A. Levine, and Associates, Opportunity in Adversity. San Francisco: Jossey-Bass, 1985.

Janice S. Green has been vice-president and academic dean of Bradford College since 1981.

*Planning was used as a mechanism to change the culture of a
university from a declining, introspective, regional institution to a
nationally prominent, entrepreneurial university.*

Turning Problems
into Opportunities:
The University of Twente

Peter A. M. Maassen, Michiel T. E. van Buchem

For many Western European institutions of higher education, the last ten
to fifteen years have constituted a remarkable period of transition. This
period has brought, indeed, some far-reaching changes, including the end
of more or less unconditional government funding of public higher
education. In some countries these changes have included a move toward greater institutional autonomy, implying at the same time a move
toward greater institutional vulnerability. On the one hand, institutional
environments have become more and more complex and uncertain, while
on the other hand institutions are expected to deal with environmental
changes more independently and actively. These developments were an
important challenge for the institutional decision makers concerned.

In this chapter one university's experience in dealing with the challenge is described: the University of Twente, located in the city of Enschede
in the eastern part of the Netherlands. On the basis of its answers to the
challenge, Twente is known in the Netherlands as the entrepreneurial
university. However, as an important element of its entrepreneurial behavior, its "intrapreneurial" activities have also received a great deal of attention inside and outside the Netherlands. The approach of Twente is, of
course, to a large extent contextually determined. Every postsecondary
institution has its own legal, political, and socioeconomic environment,
and so has Twente. Nevertheless, the proactive and sometimes aggressive
approach of this particular university contains some interesting lessons for
universities and colleges elsewhere.

NEW DIRECTIONS FOR INSTITUTIONAL RESEARCH, no. 67, Fall 1990 © Jossey-Bass Inc., Publishers

Our purpose is to explain how Twente solved a number of critical problems in the 1970s and 1980s. We want to show how the imagination and vision of a few key figures turned the problems into challenges. Special attention will be given to the important role of planning in this process—from the planning undertaken at the government's request to the university's more recent strategic planning process. Since most readers will not be familiar with higher education in the Netherlands, we start by outlining some of the specific circumstances that have influenced the development of the Twente approach.

Dutch Higher Education: Facts and Figures

Dutch higher education is readily accessible to students over seventeen years old. Anyone who has earned the appropriate secondary education diploma can enroll in one of the Dutch higher education institutions. The diversified secondary education system, with its various tracks and levels, is expected to provide adequate preparation for entering the system of higher education. In addition to thirteen research universities (of which Twente is one), Dutch higher education consists of about ninety institutions for higher vocational education and an Open University for higher distance education. Although a number of institutions are privately run, in practice all can be regarded as public institutions. In January 1988 about 425,000 students were enrolled: 170,000 in the university sector, 220,000 in the higher vocational education sector, and 35,000 in the Open University programs.

At the end of the 1980s about 90 percent of the funds for higher education and scientific research was provided by the government. The other 10 percent came mainly from teaching and research contracts, from income from services, and from revenues from patents. As a consequence of its new strategy toward higher education, the Dutch government stimulates institutions to increase their nongovernmental income gradually and thus reduce their dependency on the government.

In retrospect, the Dutch government appears to have used two basically different strategies to influence the higher education system. First, in the late 1970s and early 1980s several drastic reforms and retrenchment operations were carried out. The government regarded these reforms and cutbacks as necessary corrective policies. They included, among other things, a reform of the university education structure, a revision of the salary structure and appointment policy for university faculty, introduction of a system of conditional funding for scientific research, and a major retrenchment operation called "task reallocation and concentration" whose basic objectives were cutting the costs of the university sector, stimulating cooperation between disciplinary locations, concentrating research activities, and preventing further disintegration of the university system.

Second, starting in 1985 a different governmental approach evolved.

Now the emphasis was on relaxing the government's oversight and increasing institutional autonomy in certain areas. The main ideas behind the government's new approach were introduced in a ministerial policy paper called "Higher Education: Autonomy and Quality," referred to as the HOAK paper. Since then several aspects of these ideas have been translated into legislation and a number of policy instruments have been developed to implement the changes. The new policy gives a great deal of prominence to planning by means of dialogue. The dialogue should be based primarily on future objectives of both the government and the higher education institutions. In addition, representatives from business and other relevant societal groups should become involved in the dialogue.

The governmental and institutional objectives are to be written down in two central documents of the planning system developed as a consequence of the new policy: the government's plan (called HOOP) and the development plans of the institutions. The HOOP document is supposed to contain all of the government's higher education documents. It is designed to offer the government's image of the future of the higher education system. The institutions' development plans are to reflect their intentions, influences from their environment, and their internal activities. As an important element of the dialogue, institutions are supposed to react to the government's ideas, intentions, and expectations as expressed in the HOOP documents and vice versa. The new planning system has a biennial cycle; the HOOP document is published in the first year and the institutional plans in the second year. The first HOOP document was published in 1987 and the first institutional development plans came out in 1988 (Maassen and Van Vught, 1989).

Historical Context

The history of the University of Twente looks like the history of many other postwar public universities in Western Europe. Their inception was often the result of major political decisions on investments in R&D for the postwar reconstruction of the national economy. To support regional economic development, many of these institutions were located in the periphery of the country.

The University of Twente was established in 1961 as the Twente University of Technology. (The name was changed to University of Twente in 1986.) It bears the name of the region in which it is situated. At that time the region was dominated by nineteenth-century branches of industry such as the textile industry. The university is sited on a rural estate of a former textile baron who collaborated with the Nazis in World War II. (His rural estate was confiscated and sold to the government for one Dutch guilder to establish the university.)

The establishment of Twente by the government was largely based on expected manpower needs as perceived in the 1950s. At that time two universities of technology already existed in the Netherlands, the universities of Delft and Eindhoven, but as part of its postwar reconstruction program the government decided to set up a third university of technology. The government expected the new university to play an important role in regional economic development. Political support and lobbying activities from the Twente region convinced the minister of education and science that this particular area was the best location for the new university. Although representatives of other regions had tried to persuade the minister of the advantages of their areas as university sites, the Twente region was selected mainly because of its industrial activities.

In the national context, the new university was considered to be the proper place for introducing certain new elements in Dutch higher education:

• It was set up as the only deliberately planned university campus in the Netherlands. The buildings of other Dutch universities are more or less spread over the city in which they are located.

• Unlike the other two universities of technology, it was designed to become a "real" university with at least two academic cores: engineering and applied social sciences.

• The engineering programs should offer a considerable number of courses in the humanities and social sciences.

In 1964 the first programs were offered in mechanical engineering, electronics, and chemical engineering. About 200 students enrolled that first year. The government expected Twente's total enrollment to grow to about 4,000 students between 1964 and 1970.

Developments Since 1964

A number of expectations regarding Twente did not come true. The university was established in the Twente region for reasons of regional support and development, but by the end of the 1960s there was a lack of potential industrial partners. Major parts of the region's industry had collapsed and thus could not serve as a basis for new economic growth or symbiotic relationships, especially in the area of research. In addition, in the 1970s regional development was hardly a political issue anymore, so Twente gradually lost its status as a special institution deserving special government treatment.

A second problem arose when the other higher education institutions were able to fill a greater part of the national need for engineers than was expected. Partly as a consequence, enrollment at Twente grew less than was originally planned. In 1970 total enrollment was only about 2,000 students instead of the planned 4,000, although the infrastructure was designed for the latter number. As a result, average operational costs per student were too high and government funding, based on student numbers, was lower than expected. On top of that, overall Dutch enrollment for engineering programs dropped rather significantly in the 1970s, as it did in many European countries. Consequently, in 1978 only 600 freshmen entered Twente.

The demographic prospects too were rather threatening at the end of the 1970s. It was expected that in the 1980s the number of eighteen-year-olds would diminish 30 percent. As a consequence, the only way growth was thought possible was by offering new programs, using existing expertise, and exploiting the combination of engineering science and social sciences. Another problem for Twente was related to its lack of clear visibility in Dutch higher education. Twente had no special reputation in teaching or research and no outstanding departments, though a number of individual scholars had excellent reputations. Finally, in the early 1980s all universities in the Netherlands were confronted with the major restructuring and retrenchment operations mentioned earlier.

As a reaction to these problems, several steps were taken in the 1970s but were not really coordinated:

• Twente set up a faculty of Business Administration in 1972 and a faculty of Public Administration in 1976.

• A research emphasis was developed on biomedical technology and related areas.

• The faculties of Electronics and Applied Mathematics started a new program in informatics. Although the government was reluctant to approve this initiative, enough additional funding was raised to set up in 1981 a new faculty of Informatics and Computer Sciences.

• A program in educational technology was developed during the second half of the 1970s, and in 1978 it was approved by the government. The first courses were given in 1982.

Some of these steps were initiated by the faculties, and some were offered by the national government. The governing board of the university, however, lagged behind in this matter and initiated few of the necessary activities.

A Strategy for the 1980s

At the beginning of the 1980s, Twente was confronted with a number of serious questions. The new programs and courses offered new opportunities, but how could the existing programs and courses be balanced with the new ones in a situation where all universities had to deal with decreasing income from the Ministry of Education and Science? How could money and facilities be reallocated from the existing faculties to the new ones? How could uncertainties with respect to the level of state funding be diminished by locating other financial resources? How could problems related to the large number of tenured faculty and its negative influence on the flexibility of the university be overcome? Furthermore, at the beginning of the 1980s, the minister of education and science indicated that it was necessary, because of budgetary and other reasons, to close down a number of faculties and programs in Dutch institutions. This move, in combination with general budget cuts, increased competition and rivalry between universities. How should Twente compete in this environment?

In dealing with these problems, Twente tried to respond but lacked the overall vision and consensus on goals to set priorities regarding alternative actions. This lack was felt more strongly as a result of key changes in the university environment. The interest in technological education had increased again. Moreover, the higher vocational education institutions were claiming a new status more on a par with the universities.

In the midst of this situation, two strong personalities became members of the university's governing board. Erik Bolle, a mathematician, came to take charge of finance and planning, and Harry van den Kroonenberg, full professor in mechanical engineering, became rector of the university. In addition, a third key figure, Harry Fekkers, joined the university. He was a graduate from Twente who, after a career in municipal government, was asked by Bolle to head the university's planning office.

These three men were instrumental in developing the university between 1981 and 1988. They had different characters and played different roles. Bolle organized a thorough debate on mission and goals and acted as the main negotiator between Twente and the national government—not only with respect to funding but also to create room for the university to maneuver more independently. Van den Kroonenberg acted as the ambassador of the university. He was enthusiastic, creative, and replete with new ideas about research and education. An expert at dealing with the media, he managed to present Twente at the national level as a dynamic and entrepreneurial university. Thus he created a new image for the university. Fekkers served in the background with both a sensitivity for organizational constraints and a creativity for finding solutions to internal problems. He was the designer of a new financing system and a new planning procedure, both necessary for implementing new strategies. Although these three men were different personalities in many respects, they had one motto in common: "We don't have problems. We only have challenges and opportunities." The planning processes at Twente described in the following sections resulted largely from their efforts, imagination, and inspiration.

Planning Since 1980

The first step undertaken by Bolle and Fekkers was to develop a five-year institutional plan that responded to the government's request to all Dutch universities. This plan can best be characterized by its underlying fundamental questions: Where are we going and what is our university policy? In preparation for producing the plan, governing board members were asked for their opinions with respect to this question. Then the faculties were asked to express their opinions in the context of the macro-level statements. All statements were collected in a single document called the "yellow book."

It is easy to point out a number of mistakes in this first step—for example, there were a wide variety of perceptions, hardly a link between mission and operational management, and some contradictions in policy statements. On the whole, however, it was considered a useful exercise for several reasons. It enabled the university to

- Define a general frame of reference for governing board and university council decisions
- Seek some consistency and consensus
- Improve its image and reputation
- Unfreeze faculty thinking about directions, possible growth, and income sources.

Van den Kroonenberg contributed to this policy development by "opening windows" to local government and national industry and by hammering away at the university's mission in society: "to create a continuous flow of knowledge to society, not only by graduates, but also through an active transfer of science and technology directly into enterprises."

The second step was made in 1983. If one wants to encourage faculties to innovate, to maximize income from nongovernmental sources, to contribute to defining an institutional mission, and to encourage institutional development, give them room to maneuver. That is, give them more possibilities to deal with and more room to design their own future. In 1983 Fekkers introduced a less centralized budgeting system with more autonomy for faculties to choose their own product mix. The system was based on a cost/profit center approach. Some features of this system are

- Outputs should translate into income.
- All funds are allocated on a lump-sum basis to the faculties, which have spending freedom and can switch expenditures within general constraints.
- Faculties are encouraged to seek additional and multiple sources of funding.
- Budgeting is based on output factors rather than input factors—for example, on students who finish a program of study instead of on first-year enrollments.
- A proportion of the central budget is retained for stimulating innovation, pump priming, and resolving certain problems.

This decentralization received a lot of attention throughout Dutch higher education, for budget allocation is an important coordination mechanism for the university governing board and the university council.

As a third step, in 1984 the governing board of the university initiated development of a new institutional plan. This plan was expected to incorporate all the new developments and opportunities that had been brought about since the beginning of the 1980s, mainly as a result of the efforts of Bolle, Van den Kroonenberg, and Fekkers. Consequently the plan contained the following major goals:

- Maintain a total enrollment of 4,000 to 5,000 students
- Achieve and maintain a critical mass of faculty, staff, students, and resources in a number of disciplinary clusters
- Raise funding from multiple nongovernmental sources
- Play a more influential and responsive role in the region and in the Dutch business community through research, knowledge and technology transfer, continuing education, and contract activities—in other words, become more entrepreneurial and market oriented.

The need to increase the faculty's freedom of action has already been mentioned. To realize the policy goals, however, another set of problems had to be dealt with. These problems were related to questions about Twente's future directions in a number of areas and about translating the policy goals into day-to-day operations and budget decisions. The main problems were:

1. How to realign the faculty's thinking? Faculty in the Netherlands were not used to thinking in terms of clients, markets, and quality of output. They saw themselves as members of an academic community rather than as participants in an organization, responsible for achieving its goals, and accountable for its successes and losses.

2. How to formulate a specific mission for Twente? Too much vagueness means that there are no guidelines for strategic decisions. But too much detail might be threatening to the departments, while it also could limit creativity and innovation. If the governing board developed a mission statement, would faculty and students recognize it as relevant for them?

3. How to develop a professional strategic management approach for the university? For this one needs, among other things, professional academic and nonacademic managers. In Dutch universities there are three levels of authority: the university governing board and the university council; the faculty boards and the faculty council; and the research groups. Each level has its own decision-making power. The problems are how to stimulate these loosely coupled levels to perform management tasks they do not always recognize as their responsibility and how to establish a system of concerted activities wherever it is necessary. In other words, an approach was needed that would develop a management approach in the academic context, reward those who perform management tasks, and promote a flexible support and services system considering faculties as clients, not as opponents. Both were needed to cope with Twente's future opportunities and challenges.

University decision makers believed that these problems could best be dealt with through an adequate strategic planning process. Therefore, in 1986, an overall project was started to develop a strategic plan for Twente for the 1990s.

A Strategic Plan for the 1990s

Compared to its situation in the 1970s and early 1980s, Twente was in much better shape in 1986. First-year enrollment was 1,200 that year, the number of research-based publications had increased (and more and more were recognized as being competitive in quality), and nongovernment funding had increased in absolute and relative terms. Having dealt with the structural problems, it seemed time to make some important strategic choices concerning the future direction the university should take.

The governing board commenced the planning process with the publication of an internal report entitled "Entrepreneurial University or Scientific Enterprise?: The UT in the 1990s." This report was the subject of profound discussions with members of the university council, faculty boards, administrative directors of the faculties, and in a plenary meeting with all full professors. The reactions were quite different. They ranged from support for the attempt to clarify the university's mission and to develop institutional strategies to criticism of its contents or even strong disapproval of form, contents, and procedure. Some did not note any difference from the university's current profile, whereas others accused the governing board of selling out its basic values. One of the main criticisms was that the report proposed a slide in the direction of a vocational-oriented higher education institution. In general, the opponents of the report believed that the governing board had interfered improperly with the responsibilities of the professionals.

On the basis of these discussions, the governing board produced a new report entitled "Entrepreneurial University and Academic Enterprise." This new report also was brought up for discussion and the results were used to draft the strategic plan that was published in June 1987. This draft plan opened with a simple statement: "What is our position, what should our position be in the future, and how can we achieve this?" Trying to answer these three questions required setting priorities and making certain choices. These choices must be suitable for future activities but must also consider the university's past, its character, and its responsibilities. In addition to dealing with Twente's future, the strategic plan had to address the following parameters:

- It should offer guidelines to the various faculties with respect to the organization and implementation of education, research, and services.
- It should provide a framework for strategic decision making at the level of the governing board and the university council.

- It should be a starting point for coordination and cooperation within the university, as well as for cooperation with other institutions and organizations.
- It should be a frame of reference for defining and dividing tasks, especially where talent and resources are in short supply.

After these topics were discussed at the beginning of the document, the draft plan continued with a description of trends and future prospects for the university—particularly the relationship between scientific education and research on the one hand and society, economy, technology, and political and demographic developments on the other. In addition, the draft dealt with questions related to competition and rivalry (intrauniversity and interuniversity as well as between universities and institutes for higher vocational education) and questions regarding the quality of education and research.

In line with these considerations a future profile of the university was described in the draft. The main elements of this profile were the following:

1. The university should have two main educational cores—technical engineering and humanities—with a number of "intercore" programs.
2. Research conducted inside the university should be innovative, strategic, and multidisciplinary.
3. The educational programs of the university should be oriented toward future professional activities.
4. The university should aim at high quality in its education, research, and services.
5. Twente should be an entrepreneurial university.
6. Twente should maintain its status as a campus university, which means that study, work, housing, restaurant, cultural, social, and sport facilities are kept together on a single site.
7. The university should be a cultural, scientific, and social center with a strong regional impact based on quality, size, and international recognition.
8. The university should have a total annual enrollment of around 6,000 students.
9. Twente should increase, absolutely and relatively, the level of nongovernment funding for its education, research, and services.
10. In general, Twente should become less dependent on the government.

At the end of 1987, after a thorough debate throughout the university, the draft strategic plan was, with minor alterations, broadly accepted as a guideline for the future development of Twente.

The Nature of the Planning Process

University officials, especially Bolle and Fekkers, emphasized from the beginning that, in their eyes, the main function of university planning was not goal setting or producing a plan but bringing about changes in the culture of the university. Planning should be used to make certain controversial matters subject to discussion, to deal with prejudices, or as Fekkers used to say, "To stir up the pond." At Twente planning is regarded as a way to steer the cultural climate of the university.

As a consequence, the process is far more important than the documents. The various institutional plans outlined practical conditions for future operations. Each successive plan was expected to provide a general frame of reference for the various activities of the university and—especially the 1987 strategic plan—was based on a certain level of consensus throughout the university regarding the character of the institutional profile included in the plan.

This consensus was created through a number of what might be called circular discussions. Each segment of the university was involved on several occasions in discussing strategies, ideas, alternatives, values, and options, and the results of the discussions were used in each subsequent round. The whole planning process can be described as overlapping like roof tiles. This seems to be a very valuable way to create a planning process that fits the nature of a university and is in line with its basic characteristics, including a fragmented structure organized around knowledge areas and diffused decision-making power (Clark, 1983; Maassen and Van Vught, in press).

Another important element of the planning process at Twente was its learning aspect. Through the various cycles, not only the governing board and its staff but also the faculties got more accustomed to this planning approach where the plan is less important than the process.

In developing a planning approach suitable for Twente, university officials ran into a number of problems while trying to apply the literature on planning to their institution. The most serious problems related to two characteristics of the literature: First, nearly all of it was oriented toward North American higher education; second, only a limited amount was based on empirical studies of planning. In general, the literature on planning contained very few practical guidelines for setting up an appropriate planning system at a Dutch university.

In the second half of the 1980s a British expert in university management was asked to review the Twente planning system. His findings and recommendations were used during the strategic planning process (Davies, 1986). In addition, a presentation by an institutional researcher from California at the 9th EAIR Forum in 1987 provided valuable information on a strategic planning process at an American university. These lessons were helpful in assessing the pros and cons of the university's planning approach (Slovacek, 1988).

The Entrepreneurial University

Planning can be regarded as an important instrument in changing Twente from a purely academic, mainly internally oriented, organization into an internally and externally oriented entrepreneurial institution. The specific way in which knowledge is transferred has been a key element of Twente's entrepreneurial activities.

Knowledge is generated by people. Establishing personal contacts with representatives from trade, industry, and the government is a precarious matter. Building and maintaining a network of relations based on personal contacts is regarded by Twente as the critical factor for transferring knowledge. An important condition for transference is that partners in the network believe that their personal interests or those of their organization are strengthened when they participate actively in the network (Verschoor, 1989).

Since the end of the 1970s, Twente's governing board has tried to improve the accessibility of the university's knowledge handling processes by

- Stimulating faculties, departments, and individual professors to seek contract research projects.
- Setting up a university "science and information shop" aimed at the dissemination of knowledge and expertise to organizations and individuals that do not have research funds and have no commercial intentions. In addition, the shop aims at the inclusion of societal problems in the education and research programs of Twente. In this way it wants to increase communication and understanding between society, the scientific community, and students.
- Setting up in 1979 an industrial liaison office or "transfer center." It was the first of its kind in Dutch higher education and plays an important role in policy developments with respect to social services of the university.
- Influencing the establishment of a so-called Business Technological Center (BTC) in the immediate vicinity of the university. The BTC offers working space, facilities, and managerial know-how to starting entrepreneurs who graduated from Twente.

The Intrapreneurial University

The provisions of Dutch public law did not allow the university to undertake certain entrepreneurial activities. Twente dealt with this impediment by setting up, in 1985, a private enterprise called Technopolis Twente. The secretary of Twente was appointed as its president, and the members of the university governing board constitute its corporate board. Its main purpose is to offer a structure in which activities can be developed as spin-offs of regular university tasks such as research, teaching, and social service. Some of the activities carried out by Technopolis Twente are

1. The establishment of the International Conference and Study Center (ICSC). The center is located at the heart of the university campus and is especially designed for conferences, courses, and seminars. ICSC not only offers accommodations but can also play an active role in the organization of congresses and the like. Furthermore, it can design tailor-made seminars and courses for companies and other organizations.

2. The founding of Biomass Technology Group (BTG Ltd.) so that the biomass gasification unit (faculty of chemical technology) could develop activities in the Third World.

3. The establishment of the Educational Computer Consortium (ECC Ltd.) for development and evaluation of educational software and courseware for several levels of education. It also serves as a national information center for educational technology.

4. The development of Office Center Technopolis, where 4,000 square meters of office space was built both for the Educational Computer Consortium and the various contract research activities of Twente's faculties and departments.

In Technopolis Twente every industrial spin-off can be accommodated. It offers the university the possibility to profit from all incentive measures, bounty systems, grants, and state aids that exist in the Netherlands, ranging from investment grants and wage aids to development credits.

Present Position of Twente

How did things work out for Twente? Where did the various activities lead? At the start of the 1990s the university has ten strong, viable faculties: mechanical engineering, business administration, electronics, chemical technology, applied physics, applied mathematics, computer science, public administration, applied educational science, and philosophy of science and technology. Of these, the last six are the largest in enrollment and research efforts in the Netherlands or are totally unique. In addition, Twente has developed a number of successful multidisciplinary programs—for example, biomedical engineering, mathematics for economics, ergonomics, higher education policy studies, and technology for developing countries.

Twente has, in 1990, some 1,600 freshmen and a total enrollment of 6,500 students. It has a large number of postgraduate courses. It has increased its research efforts by almost 100 percent compared to 1980, while the increase for the Dutch higher education system as a whole is about 50 percent. The quality of its education and research has been reviewed satisfactorily by external committees in recent years. Social service and consultancy have been accepted more and more by the faculty as profitable tasks at Twente and have improved its internal management.

These developments were, of course, influenced by many factors. It was certainly not just through its specific planning approach, for example, that Twente has become a successful institution. Nonetheless, the combined vision and imagination of a number of key figures who turned problems into opportunities—through adapting planning to the university instead of the other way around—certainly has contributed to the fact that Twente can step into the next decade with more self-assurance and trust than it had ten years ago.

References

Clark, B. R. *The Higher Education System: Academic Organization in Cross-National Perspective.* Berkeley: University of California Press, 1983.

Davies, J. L. "Review of the Planning System of the University of Twente." Internal report, University of Twente, 1986.

Maassen, P.A.M., and Van Vught, F. A. *Dutch Higher Education in Transition: Policy-Issues in Higher Education in the Netherlands.* Culemborg, Netherlands: LEMMA, 1989.

Maassen, P.A.M., and Van Vught, F. A. "Strategic Planning in Higher Education." In B. R. Clark and G. Neave (eds.), *Encyclopaedia of Higher Education.* London: Pergamon, in press.

Slovacek, S. P. "Strategic Planning and Self-Study." In H. R. Kells and F. A. Van Vught (eds.), *Self-Regulation, Self-Study and Program Review in Higher Education.* Culemborg, Netherlands: LEMMA, 1988.

Verschoor, F. "The Twente Entrepreneurial and Intrapreneurial Experience." In *Proceedings of the Sixth International Meeting of University Administrators.* College Park: University of Maryland, 1989.

Peter A. M. Maassen is associate director of the Dutch Center for Higher Education Policy Studies (CHEPS) at the University of Twente.

Michiel T. E. van Buchem is deputy registrar of the University of Twente and former chair of Twente's planning office.

*The flexibility of an issue-oriented approach to planning helped a
healthy institution respond to internal and external challenges.*

Issue-Oriented Planning:
Essex Community College

Philip M. Ringle, Frederick W. Capshaw

As it entered the 1980s, Essex Community College, located near Baltimore,
faced many of the same issues confronting other higher education institutions. Projected declines in traditional-aged students, increased competition
for funding, heightened awareness of the needs of special and underrep-
resented populations, and an extended state role in governance were occur-
ring simultaneously. Campus leaders recognized that these issues could not
be ignored.

The importance of institutional responsiveness to challenges posed by
the external environment has been heavily emphasized in the planning
literature. This literature offers much useful advice on how to conduct
mission reviews, identify institutional strengths and weaknesses, assess the
external environment, and construct alternative future scenarios. Less has
been written about the planning required to advance an institution that
has determined it is healthy, responsive to its mission, and does not need
major redirection or restructuring of its programs and services. Essex's
experiences in the last decade illustrate how, at a healthy institution with a
clearly defined mission, issue-oriented planning has been the key to continuing health and vitality.

Adaptability and flexibility have characterized Essex's response to its
issues and challenges. While these terms may suggest an absence of planning, the approach at Essex incorporates the elements of traditional planning systems that are relevant to every dynamic organization. The Essex
approach combines the most useful elements of existing models with the
recognition that no single model will be effective if it ignores the unique
character of the institution or the nature of the issues it confronts.

NEW DIRECTIONS FOR INSTITUTIONAL RESEARCH, no. 67, Fall 1990 © Jossey-Bass Inc., Publishers   69

Background

From its establishment in 1957 until the late 1970s, Essex Community College had experienced many years of growth and prosperity. By the 1979–80 academic year, full-time equivalent enrollment exceeded 5,300, mostly in credit programs that served over 9,300 area residents. The student body resembled that of many suburban two-year colleges: 59 percent were females, 73 percent were enrolled part-time, and 45 percent were over twenty-five years of age. State aid, based on full-time equivalent enrollment, provided the largest portion of funding (38 percent) for the college's $11.5 million operating budget, followed by support from Baltimore County (34 percent) and income from tuition and fees (26 percent). The college's 168 full-time faculty members taught nearly two-thirds of the credit program.

As a public open-door community college, Essex embraced the organizing principles of the comprehensive community college:

(1) commitment to be different from traditional higher education through emphasis on access, convenience, low cost, and location of services; (2) emphasis on two-year [transfer programs and] paraprofessional training; (3) reliance on quantitative growth as [one] adequate [indicator] to measure success; (4) commitment to personalized education through emphasis on teaching as the primary institutional activity; and (5) commitment to civic education as reflected in efforts to diminish the institutional barriers between these colleges and the communities they served through community based education [Eaton, 1988, p. 2].

To carry out its mission, the college offered five general programs: transfer programs, career/vocational programs, certificate programs, continuing education courses, and community service and cultural enrichment activities. In the late 1970s and early 1980s, as the college experienced the first enrollment declines in its history, struggled with the consequences of high inflation and less generous funding, and enrolled increasing numbers of underprepared students, many administrators and faculty wondered whether it would be able to maintain the quality and comprehensiveness of its diverse offerings.

In retrospect, the somewhat gloomy predictions of the early 1980s may have been fortunate for Essex. They provided a context for serious reviews of the college's mission and focused attention on emerging issues. By the end of the decade, the college had not only reaffirmed its commitment to its organizing principles but had also strengthened many of its major programs and services. During the 1989–90 academic year, the college served approximately 8,000 full-time equivalent credit and noncredit students, 40 percent more than four years earlier. While the demographic profile of its student body was largely unchanged, noncredit students now comprised almost one-third of the total enrollment. The college's budget had more than tripled, reaching approximately $26 million in fiscal year 1989–90, with Baltimore County now providing the largest share of income (47 percent). Moreover, because of its experiences with issue-oriented planning, the institution is better prepared to deal with emerging challenges such as educating increasing numbers of transfer students and providing tailor-made programming for local business and industry.

A Planning Dilemma

To employ a planning approach successfully, the planner must appraise the internal and external environment of the institution (Steiner, 1979). To understand the planning approaches successful at Essex Community College, one must consider both the internal and external environment for planning. This environment includes the college's basic character, which may not be easily discernible. As at other institutions, demographic information and program descriptions do not express Essex's full character. This "character" is more accurately derived from considering the institution's implicit mission, formal and informal value systems, history, administrative structure, and opportunities for change.

The history of Essex Community College is rich in its traditions of shared governance, participatory management, and faculty involvement in decision making. While some have suggested that community colleges are run primarily by administrators, faculty at Essex are active in a broad spectrum of planning and policy-making activities. Many faculty and staff participate in mission reviews conducted by the college's Middle States reaccreditation task forces, its planning committee, and its standing governance bodies. Each review has reaffirmed the mission of the institution and, with the exception of several issues needing attention, confirmed the college's essential health. The appropriateness of the mission was further reinforced by external funding agencies, businesses and industries served by the college, student and graduate survey results, and reviews of statewide research data. The president, his staff, the faculty, and other key constituency groups, implicitly and explicitly, made the strategic decision not to restructure or redirect the institution. Instead they decided to address issues attracting campus-wide concern or affecting several constituencies, to improve targeted services and programs, and to emphasize institutional activities that would enhance achievement of the college's mission.

Given the college's traditions and circumstances, developing useful approaches for planning was not easy. Issues affecting the basic nature and future of the organization did not often require institution-wide attention. Yet the administration and governance bodies recognized the need to continue the emphasis on shared governance and participatory management and to include as many individuals and groups on campus as possible in addressing key institutional issues. Though no strategic redirection was called for and the institution was healthy in terms of enrollment, funding, and external indicators, the college needed to address issues in ways that reflected its basic character and involved all campus constituencies whose participation was required to develop and implement sound educational plans.

The issue-oriented approach to planning that emerged at Essex involved adapting strategic planning concepts to the institution's essential character. The problem of accommodating Essex Community College's institutional character within a planning process was addressed by building on the college's flexibility and using different planning approaches for different issues.

The processes for addressing the issues confronting Essex were not predetermined. The nature of the issue determined the approach. Two major categories of issues emerged. One set of issues was characterized by externally mandated data and information requirements, a need for direction from one major service unit on the campus, a reliance on technical expertise, and tasks within the scope of one department or division. Structured and centralized planning processes (within the administrative purview of one department or division) were effective in resolving these issues. The second set of major issues was more complex. These issues needed diverse input from many divisions and departments, had less clearly defined boundaries, and lacked an organizational entity responsible for implementing solutions. This second category required more decentralized and fluid planning processes. The following sections describe how the college applied different approaches to different issues and illustrate why flexible planning approaches are important within the framework of issue-oriented planning.

Issues Addressed by Centralized and Structured Processes

Management Information Systems. Essex Community College's management information systems are coordinated by a data processing department with responsibility for both administrative and academic computing. In the early 1980s, many faculty and administrators were expressing considerable concern about the way in which the college's information needs were being addressed. A long-range plan was needed to guide the future development of the college's computing and management information systems.

The college's approach to developing its management information systems reflected both the need to obtain input from several campus constituencies and the relatively technical nature of the issue. A planning process that incorporated many of the steps prescribed for traditional, institutionwide approaches to planning was developed. The planning team included representatives of areas affected by the use of management information systems. This team used structured interviews and conducted a campus-wide assessment of computer hardware and software capabilities and needs to compile the information needed to prepare a five-year plan. The plan that emerged from the committee's work established priorities, outlined implementation strategies, and provided preliminary cost estimates and timetables for hardware and software acquisition, computer program development, and staff training. It also addressed important issues related to the coordination of instructional, academic, and administrative computing.

The plan provided the foundation for obtaining a five-year Title III grant that allowed the college to develop major new systems for finance, financial aid, personnel, academic administration, and grants management. Each year, the data processing center translates the strategic plan into an operational plan that establishes priorities, sets goals, and recommends expenditures for the fiscal year. The center's staff coordinates this phase of planning activity for the entire institution. Essential input is obtained from all campus constituencies, but the scope of work undertaken, the priority of the work, and resources and staffing are all centrally determined.

This two-stage approach, which provides broadly based input for a centrally coordinated function, has been effective in developing a management information system because the college community recognizes the need for technical expertise and a coordinated institution-wide process for managing information. The location of resources within one unit facilitated the centralized approach to implementation once the plan was adopted.

Budget Development. Essex Community College's approach to building its annual budget provides another example of the appropriateness and usefulness of employing relatively formal planning methods for certain issues. At Essex, the budget process begins at the departmental level and then advances through regular organizational channels to the president's office. Opportunities for the college's governance bodies to provide input are provided at various stages in the process. At each stage, new programs, major new endeavors, and operational goals for the upcoming year are presented and priorities for resource allocation are discussed. After the president and his staff receive the proposed budgets for each major functional area, they make decisions regarding the total amount to be requested and the specific items to be included in the college's final budget proposal to the county executive. This pyramidal process involves a participatory approach that is consistent with the college's fundamental values, results in a consensus on departmental goals, and allows budget allocations to parallel the college's operational plan for the next fiscal year.

Consensus seeking and compromise are more prevalent, and more important to campus morale, in the budget building process than in the process used to plan the college's management information system, but fewer individuals make the final decisions. The participatory process is designed to provide the decision makers with the most comprehensive and detailed information available.

External Resource Development. In 1984, Essex's president foresaw that finding external resources was important to the college's future vitality. Upon the retirement of the college's director of facilities development, the president recognized an opportunity to restructure the college's administrative organization and expand its external resource capabilities. With feedback from campus constituencies, the president created a fourth deanship to complement the deans of instruction, student services, and administrative services. The newly created position of dean of planning and development was assigned major responsibilities for institutional advancement and support.

To initiate the expanded external resource development effort, the dean met with faculty and staff in each division and formulated a list of topics that were of interest to the campus but for which funding was not available from traditional sources. He then prepared a "grant development plan" that matched the areas of college interest with potential sources of funding. Grants were used, in much the same way R&D funds are used in industry, to develop new programs, expand existing services, or supplement needed services. Grants also were used to encourage faculty creativity in areas of their interest or expertise. As a result of this process, grant revenues have grown by over 100 percent during the past five years. The college's efforts were furthered by adding a director of development and a director of corporate and foundation relations and by increasing attention to the activities of the Essex Community College Foundation.

The college's planning for external resource development represented yet one more approach to institutional issues affecting the institution's future vitality and responsiveness. In this instance, the plan developed from the vision of the president and from a reorganization that was advanced primarily by administrative offices. There was no expression of interest from other constituencies, no pressing external issues to respond to, no inertia to overcome. Lengthy debate was not required, and issues of turf were rarely germane to the problems under consideration. The planning data to support the changes, and the final form of the response, were developed and implemented very quickly and without extensive discussion.

Program and Facilities Development. Further examples of issues that respond to a relatively formal planning approach include those that involve external agencies and have mandated data requirements. At Essex, new program development is regulated by an elaborate monitoring system developed by the Maryland State Board for Community Colleges. Initially, the impetus for a program proposal can result from faculty interest, community input, or administrative encouragement. The location of the institution also influences program development. Essex has developed strong and comprehensive allied health programs because of the college's proximity to a large hospital complex.

Once a new program is deemed consistent with the college's mission and the development of a formal program proposal is agreed to by the administration, a series of research studies and data gathering techniques are employed by the academic program development staff and the office of institutional research. Typical studies include Developing a Curriculum (DACUM) meetings with industry representatives, surveys of employment needs, reviews of similar training at other institutions, and analyses of employment trends, discipline cost projections, space requirements, and equipment needs. This highly structured system has worked well to ensure the campus and the state that, based on standardized statewide data, community college resources are being used efficiently and in the areas of greatest program need.

Planning for new facilities also follows a regimented process dictated by county and state regulations. New buildings are proposed to the county and state for funding. Once funding is scheduled, the college appoints a building committee that selects an architect and a site, develops educational specifications, and reviews the architect's design, development, and construction drawings. Renovation of existing spaces is a highly structured process as well. Each year, the cost center administrators on the campus submit a list of required renovations and space needs to their dean. The deans then identify, in consultation with their staffs, priority requests for their areas of responsibility and submit a list of needs to the dean of planning and development and dean of administrative services. These two offices then estimate costs for each project and bring a list of projects to the president's staff. The list is put in priority order, and a final list is discussed with campus constituents. When budget allocations are received, project funding proceeds in the priority order until funding is exhausted.

New program development and facilities planning follow well-defined processes and are typical of planning issues requiring a formal approach. Issues that deal with the allocation of resources (capital or operating) lend themselves more easily to traditional planning models. As noted earlier, however, less formal approaches are often more effective when issues affect the basic character of the institution, cross organizational and departmental lines, or represent new initiatives.

Issues Addressed by Decentralized Processes

Developmental Education Reform. By the early 1980s, Essex's faculty had developed a reputation for excellence in a number of disciplines and the college had won national and even international recognition. However, an awareness began to emerge that work remained to be done in some academic areas fundamental to the approved mission. In 1982, a survey of the faculty revealed that 70 percent believed that the college admitted unprepared students. Fully 50 percent of the faculty thought that the college was not doing a good job in bringing such students up to college level. While the college had a number of departmental requirements and courses in developmental education, nothing approaching a developmental program existed. The college recognized that developmental education touched the values, beliefs, and educational philosophy of the institution. If changes were to be implemented, new approaches that would reconcile the broad range of faculty views were needed.

The dean of instruction consulted with the college governance organization responsible for academic matters to create an ad hoc committee, with extensive representation, to explore developmental education. This committee's composition of nineteen members was designed to involve all points of view of those active in, and interested in, developmental education. While the committee's size threatened to be burdensome, its composition ensured support and consensus among key players early in the process. This committee began meeting in November 1982 and finished its work in June 1984. In addition to examining current offerings at Essex, the committee reviewed current literature in the field, judged the Essex approach against other models, and finally prepared a set of recommendations covering six areas ranging from mandatory assessment and placement to a new administrative structure. The report served as both a strategic and a tactical plan, providing direction and context for program improvement in developmental education at Essex throughout the 1980s.

Developmental education has been supported by a significant increase in research services. Statistical reports describe compliance with the assessment policy, local norms for the assessment instruments, relationships between assessment scores and grades, enrollment information on developmental students, utilization of support services, and student progress and completion rates in developmental courses. Supported by this research, developmental education has made steady and significant progress throughout the ensuing period.

Essex's approach to the issue of developmental education teaches a number of lessons. It suggests that expressions of faculty opinion can be a starting point for significant reform, even when the approach may run counter to institutional traditions. The ad hoc structure allowed leadership in developmental education to evolve and resulted in a plan that has guided the college for a decade. The administration played a key supporting role for academic change not only by providing enabling structures but by seeking both external support through a Title III grant and internal support through released time, computing, and research services. Most important, the faculty itself came to understand, through its study, the value of college-wide structures in developmental education and opted for a radical departure from previous practices dictated by departmental control.

Revision of General Education. The Essex experience in addressing general education exhibits important similarities and differences from its experience with developmental education. In 1981, after several years of intense debate, the college adopted a set of distribution requirements as the foundation of its general education program. This approach specified certain academic areas in which students must complete required numbers of credits to earn an associate of arts degree and then allowed students to select from large groups of courses within each area. As is usual in such circumstances, academic divisions viewed themselves as winners or losers in the allotment of general education courses to be taken within the division.

While such an approach certainly has its merits, at Essex, as at many two-year and four-year institutions, insufficient attention was devoted to the ways in which individual courses met general education objectives. As a result, the college gradually experienced a proliferation of courses deemed acceptable for general education requirements. In the humanities and arts division, for example, eighty-four different courses could be used to meet a 6-credit distribution requirement. A similar situation existed in the social science division. Since the existing plan had been arrived at after prolonged debate, there was little energy for change and a prevailing desire to leave well enough alone.

At the same time a national dialogue began within the higher education community on the goals of general education. In the midst of this national dialogue, at Essex there was continuing debate over a number of related issues: higher standards, more structure, replacement of distribution requirements with a more purposeful integrated core approach, the purposes of liberal education, reemphasis of skills, and the need to promote awareness of cross-cultural and minority contributions. These discussions frequently led faculty to serious conversations about the college's academic mission and the needs of its student body. While all of these issues emerged independently during considerations of courses and programs at the college, no comprehensive approach under the rubric of general education was undertaken.

Clearly, the college needed a mechanism to plan for general education. The dean of instruction met with faculty leaders to discuss possible structures for the planning process. Since the topic was too far-reaching to be dealt with by existing governance or planning structures, an ad hoc committee was agreed upon. All parties were assured that if, after a study, the committee chose to support the existing system of distribution requirements, no changes would be strong-armed by the administration. Assurances also were given that if divisional enrollments fell drastically as a result of changes, faculty would be cross-trained to teach in other disciplines or in new interdisciplinary courses so that no one would lose a job because of changes in the general education requirements.

The planning process used to address the general education issue was developed over the course of several months and included mechanisms designed to achieve consensus such as open meetings, workshops, seminars, and surveys. As this work progressed, the college accepted responsibility for a review of all courses meeting the distribution requirements. Later, discussions centered on the merits of requiring interdisciplinary core courses specifically designed to meet general education objectives, an issue that is not fully resolved. Essex's approach to general education helped the college obtain a major grant from the National Endowment for the Humanities to support faculty involvement in course development and revision. Faculty across campus are involved in what they see as the most important development on campus in many years, and many are submitting applications to teach the pilot versions of the new interdisciplinary core courses in the fall of 1990.

The differences in dealing with developmental education and general education demonstrate the need for flexibility in dealing with issues that respond to less formal approaches. Resolving the issue of general education involved a threat to current departmental offerings and, therefore, necessitated attention to concerns about job security. Without the initial administrative assurance about guaranteed future employment, the debate would have quickly degenerated into a battle over turf, not pedagogy. This issue required the administration to provide the initial impetus for work on the issue. Because of the perceived effect on employment, and the potential negative impact on discipline offerings, no campus constituency took the advocacy position on this issue. The far-reaching effect of potential changes demanded skillful political maneuvering, and the planning evolved sequentially rather than from a predetermined blueprint.

These differences shaped a different general planning process that enabled the institution to advance the general education initiative without turf battles and hardening of adversarial positions. As explained by Cynthia Hardy, the process demonstrates incremental turnaround:

> Incremental turnaround enables administrators to act opportunistically instead of heavy-handedly. It allows universities to respond to environmental changes and to work toward new priorities, albeit at a more sedate pace than the business literature would advocate. Thus, the plans of administrators mesh with the culture of the university rather than jeopardize it, and plans will emerge from the implementation process in a more viable form. Incremental turnaround depends on more than the analytic skills promoted in the strategic planning and turnaround literature; however, it also requires an intimate knowledge of how the institution works and of the political skills necessary to intervene effectively [Hardy, 1987, p. 18].

The issues of developmental education and general education would have less satisfactory outcomes if the same methods were employed—or, even worse, if more structured processes were used.

Continuing Education. From the founding of the college in 1957 until the early 1970s, little attention was given to continuing education. Most offerings in the mid seventies were nontraditional versions of traditional courses. By the outset of the 1980s, offerings were becoming increasingly focused on personal development and job-related skills. While questions of identity were still somewhat unresolved within the continuing education office, college officials became more concerned about Essex's obligation to respond to community needs through entrepreneurial efforts and to view continuing education as one of the offices most suited for this purpose. In the course of this process, continuing education offerings were redefined as being almost entirely noncredit and responsibility for nontraditional credit offerings was moved to the academic divisions.

A number of organizational and procedural practices needed revision in order to maximize both quality and responsiveness. While continuing education was growing rapidly in response to community needs, a planning mechanism was needed to ensure that it would continue to respond to changing demands from the community and the college. To remain consistent with the approved mission of the college, a list of strategic decisions was advanced by the continuing education office and promoted by the administration of the college. The decisions that would determine college responsiveness included the following:

- All offerings had to fall clearly within the college's mission and fill a community service need.
- Programs and courses had to pay for themselves.
- New opportunities would not be pursued if they resulted in overburdening a staff that is already working at near maximum capacity.
- Since the range of defined needs in the community is beyond the capacity of any single institution, the college would focus its efforts in such areas as business, business technologies, and allied health where strong credit programs and natural links to the community exist.

Overall, while the college has not determined its continuing education courses and programs through a traditional central planning approach, it has moved with clear direction to provide an increasing range of needed services to the local community in such a way as to add to the resources of the institution. A formal plan was believed to be too restrictive for continuing education, which requires rapid responses to opportunities. A planning approach that judges opportunities within the context of defined operating principles has enabled the college to respond appropriately to community needs.

Lessons Learned

Each issue described above involved a set of circumstances that, on the Essex campus, argued for unique planning and research responses. The college's mission had been reaffirmed and the college was viewed as basically healthy and responsive to its community. The driving force for planning was the need to refine, expand, and improve institutional functioning in response to emerging issues. The nature of those issues required different approaches to planning. The flexibility of the institution in developing and applying these different approaches was a key to successful issue-oriented planning. In defining an issue, certain factors were especially relevant: who was affected by the issue, whether the issue crossed traditional campus departments and divisions, the extent to which the issue was capable of challenging the institution's self-concept, how potent the issue was for the future of the campus, whether or not there was a campus "champion" for the issue, what resources could be committed, and finally, the climate the administration could provide for encouraging open and honest debate of the issue. Gerald Zaltman describes the viewpoints of the manager of change in the following passage: "The manager of educational change can keep his perspective flexible if he views the specific organizational context from five analytical viewpoints: (1) the organizational climate, (2) the nature of the organization's environment, (3) the relationship between system and environment, (4) the characteristics of the individuals involved in the change process and/or affected by it, and (5) the nature (type and attributes) of the intended change(s)" (1977, p. 16). In addition to a flexible perspective, the skilled planner needs to challenge certain assumptions underlying planning. On the community college campus, planning approaches may be more effective if they are based on the nature of an issue. Each issue, in fact, redefines the context and, therefore, the process for planning.

Mature institutions continue to be affected by decisions made by their founders such as site selection, initial hiring strategies, and vision. At such institutions, planning is not seen as a unique activity but as part of normal administrative processes. Their traditional approaches usually have facilitated annual processes and responded to information demands from government agencies. They also have demonstrated effectiveness in addressing major institutional issues, particularly those with immediate implications for substantial resource commitment.

For other issues, institutions need to recognize that planning occurs within a range of formats. Creating an environment conducive to planning and encouraging a "planful" attitude is more important than developing a highly structured approach. As John Bryson notes, "It is strategic thinking and acting that are important, not strategic planning. Indeed, if any particular approach to strategic planning gets in the way of strategic thought and action, the planning approach should be scrapped" (1988, p. 2). Planning is most successful where it takes into account institutional character and builds upon a broad-based mechanism for achieving consensus. Successful planning can be advanced by a shared hope for improvement that touches the idealism of dedicated professionals while addressing their realistic concern for security.

While an initial impetus for planned change may come from external sources, faculty, administrators, or the CEO, leadership is vital in promoting awareness of a need for change, creating a sense of responsibility and reassurance, judging institutional character, and recognizing areas of potential gain. Equally important is the manager's ability to know where the impetus and expertise for issue resolution reside. As Bryson suggests, "Decisions are handled individually below the corporate level because such decentralization is politically expedient—corporate leaders should reserve their political clout for crucial decisions. Decentralization also is necessary since often only those closest to decisions have enough information to make good ones" (1988, p. 40).

Propositional logic usually is much more effective than preemptive logic in the early phases of addressing institutional issues (Ringle and Savickas, 1983). Thus, rather than preempting the open exchange of ideas, the use of propositional logic—which encourages asking questions, stimulating thinking, circulating information, and engaging campus leaders in informal conversations—is a critical activity for managing the planning process. Dillard (1989, p. 16) suggests that "the reason not to perfect a work as it progresses is that, concomitantly, original work fashions a form the true shape of which it discovers only as it proceeds, so the early strokes are useless, however fine their sheen." The same sense of creative development is relevant to planning. While structured planning has an important place on campus, it must be balanced by an awareness of possibilities internally and externally (Schmidtlein and Milton, 1989). In contexts requiring entrepreneurship, institutions may function within a general framework in which guiding principles enable them to respond effectively to external opportunity.

Flexibility promotes excellence and vitality by leaving the future to some degree open-ended in order to explore possible futures and develop contingency plans to address alternatives. Each institution has a unique character and a value system that determines the way it will behave and on what issues it will focus. These values are not necessarily made public by the traditional information systems proposed for planning. In fact, highly codified and routine methods for developing plans may obstruct change. Planning is a number of distinct processes, and integrating these processes into the normal administrative and management activity ensures that decisions about planned change will be shared, discussed, and implemented (Milton and Ringle, 1989).

Comprehensive community colleges, like other institutions of higher education, often struggle with internal and external pressure to define and redefine their mission based on current need and historical commitment. Planning approaches and research methodologies that are characterized by flexibility can increase the institution's ability to respond to emerging needs and to maintain high standards of excellence.

References

Bryson, J. M. *Strategic Planning for Public and Nonprofit Organizations.* San Francisco: Jossey-Bass, 1988.

Dillard, A. *The Writing Life.* New York: Harper & Row, 1989.

Eaton, J. S. (ed.). *Colleges of Choice.* New York: Macmillan, 1988.

Hardy, C. "Turnaround Strategies in Universities." *Planning in Higher Education,* 1987, *16* (1), 9–21.

Milton, T., and Ringle, P. "Prescriptions Versus Realities in Institutional Planning." Paper presented at Society for College and University Planners Conference, Denver, Colorado, 1989.

Ringle, P., and Savickas, M. "Administrative Leadership: Planning and Time Perspective." *Journal of Higher Education,* 1983, *54* (6), 649–661.

Schmidtlein, F. A., and Milton, T. H. "Campus Planning in the United States: Perspectives from a Nation-Wide Study." *Planning for Higher Education,* 1989, *17* (3), 1–19.

Zaltman, G., Florio, D. H., and Sikorski, L. A. *Dynamic Educational Change: Models, Strategies, Tactics, and Management.* New York: Free Press, 1977.

Philip M. Ringle is dean of planning and development at Essex Community College in Baltimore County, Maryland.

Frederick W. Capshaw, formerly dean of instruction at Essex Community College, is president of North Hennepin Community College in Brooklyn Park, Minnesota.

Planning practices must be congruent with college and university decision processes. Issues with differing characteristics require different planning processes.

Responding to Diverse Institutional Issues: Adapting Strategic Planning Concepts

Frank A. Schmidtlein

Each of the five institutions described in the preceding chapters confronted, and successfully adapted to, different challenges during the past decade. Each employed planning practices that reflected its unique history, its basic character, and the nature of its particular issues and concerns. This chapter analyzes their experiences, focusing on several aspects of planning that have received too little attention in the literature. These include the relationship of planning to other institutional decision processes, planning's dependence on institutional circumstances, and its interactions with the characteristics of issues and concerns. This analysis, and findings from a National Center for Postsecondary Governance and Finance (NCPGF) institutional planning study (Schmidtlein and Milton, 1989), are then used to provide insights and suggestions for improving planning practices at academic institutions.

What Is Planning?

The colleges and universities discussed in this volume engaged in a highly diverse set of processes aimed at improving their prospects for success. This diversity poses several questions. First, how does one distinguish planning from other decision processes employed by these institutions? Long before contemporary notions of formal planning emerged, colleges and universities made decisions on alternatives and directions based on assessments of their situations and capabilities. If planning is a distinct function, it should be distinguishable from other forms of organizational decision making. Wildavsky (1973), viewing the inclusiveness of contemporary definitions of planning, has suggested that "if planning is everything, maybe it's nothing."

Each chapter supports the view that planning is a separate concept but not necessarily a distinct process. All of the institutions needed to determine their own unique character and the directions in which they wished to proceed—in other words, they needed to plan. However, the processes they employed varied considerably from institution to institution and from issue to issue. All emphasized the importance of flexible approaches, questioned the effectiveness of rigidly structured processes, and noted the difficulty of specifically attributing institutional success to formal planning. Their experiences appear to support Wildavsky's contention that planning is part of a variety of institutional decision-making activities.

Second, assuming that one can define planning as a distinct function, is it the most effective means for making institutional decisions? Some theories of decision making conflict with formal planning notions. Among these are the "incremental" decision-making theories described by Lindblom (1959, 1968) and others, the "garbage can" theory of decision making proposed by Cohen, March, and Olsen (1972), and the contrasts of "marketplace" with "planning" concepts of decision making by Etzioni (1967) and Schmidtlein (1973). From a less scientific perspective, people have consulted astrologers and oracles and prayed for guidance.

While all the contributors recognize the potential usefulness of giving systematic attention to planning, they also emphasize creating and fostering an entrepreneurial climate and warn against rigidly formal processes. They describe, in some circumstances, using formal planning that fosters coherent, institution-wide vision and direction while in other circumstances they avoid formal processes in order to promote individual initiative and minimize procedural costs.

The ambiguity of many planning definitions, the problems encountered in trying to apply formal prescriptions, and the criticisms of assumptions underlying planning have led some to try integrating planning notions into broader approaches to institutional decision making, rather than viewing them as separate processes. They discuss concepts of "strategic management" and "strategic decision making" and describe planning as learning. Chaffee (1985) has surveyed the evolution of these concepts, focusing on strategy as a more inclusive notion than planning. She traces views of strategy in the business world from "linear" models, to "adaptive" models, and more recently, to "interpretative" models. Proponents of these new ideas suggest that they will help colleges and universities design more effective planning processes.

The five case studies appear to support the contention that effective planning in colleges and universities is more complex and more diverse than has been suggested. Dooris and Lozier describe the evolution of planning at Penn State, leading to the current "strategic management" or "issue management" approach that seeks to integrate planning "into the everyday management of the institution." Dunn notes Tufts' transition from a formal, separate planning process to a more issue-specific, less formally structured, entrepreneurial approach that is more consistent with the president's decision-making style. All five institutions deliberately encourage entrepreneurship. Bradford, Twente, and Tufts stress planning as a means to alter their organizational culture rather than as a detailed blueprint for decisions. Planning provides a context for discussion and reshaping perceptions. Both Penn State and Essex, public institutions with well-established missions, were devoting planning attention to issues that helped focus their planning efforts rather than attempting comprehensive planning. The other three institutions, to differing degrees, have reshaped their basic mission, employing processes tailored for that purpose. However, planning in all of these institutions took many forms in order to accommodate institutional character, circumstances, and issues.

Relating Planning to Institutional Character

The literature on higher education planning stresses the importance of adapting planning practices to the institution's unique characteristics (Schmidtlein and Milton, 1990). However, most planning prescriptions do not describe differing institutional characteristics and cultures or their implications for designing planning processes. These case studies reinforce the wisdom of adapting planning processes to institutional character and shed light on their effects on planning.

Adapting Planning to Academic Decision Patterns. In colleges and universities, decisions on academic issues are usually the domain of the faculty. However, administrators exercise primary budgetary power and can modify or veto new academic initiatives because of financial implications or mission incompatibility. Administrators also have primary responsibility for ensuring that institutions comply with legal and managerial requirements and for dealing with external demands. Consequently, implementing academic decisions requires varying degrees of consultation and consensus among faculty and administrators and among staff at various levels.

All five case studies illustrate the importance of faculty involvement and leadership in planning that deals with academic issues. These institutions recognize that planning decisions on academic matters are unlikely to be implemented if they lack faculty support. Given this central role of faculty in academic decisions, the case studies also illustrate that developing a culture of faculty initiative is an important condition for timely response to academic opportunities and threats. A closer examination is needed of institutions that have promoted faculty entrepreneurship to discover how it was accomplished. Furthermore, the case studies show that different types of academic decisions require different blends of faculty and administrative leadership and involvement. The implications of these differences are assessed at the end of the chapter.

The Role of Institutional Histories and Cultures. Ringle and Capshaw have observed that every institution "has a unique character and a value system that determines the way it will behave and on what issues it will focus." At their college, this caveat was recognized explicitly by both faculty and administrators. Thus, Essex Community College's strong tradition of shared governance was accommodated by allowing faculty, with administrative support, to shape and carry out planning processes dealing with major academic concerns. Penn State also integrated planning processes into its institutional culture, slowly modifying behavior and expectations. As noted by Dooris and Lozier, maintaining continuity in the people and experiences involved in planning contributed to its success at Penn State.

At Bradford, Twente, and Tufts, new leaders believed that their institution's culture was inconsistent with long-term institutional interests. They wanted to create a more entrepreneurial climate and were willing to take the risks involved in trying to make major changes in mission or direction. One ingredient in their success may have been the careful attention given to modifying faculty perceptions and modes of thought. Maassen and van Buchem describe the efforts to give Twente's faculty more freedom of action and the need to "stir up the pond," while Dunn notes that Tufts' president encourages faculty to undertake new and different activities. Green has spoken of the need to create a new self-image at Bradford, one that generates optimism and promotes a sense of faculty "ownership." She also describes efforts to remove symbols of the old culture and notes how slowly public perceptions change.

Findings from the NCPGF study also confirm the importance of meshing the planning with institutional culture. In a number of institutions, planning that appeared inconsistent with institutional modes of behavior had minimal impact or did not persist for more than one or two cycles. Often, the arrival of a new president led to the start of new planning processes. Perhaps earlier processes were not sufficiently "institutionalized" or the concerns of the new president required a different approach.

Adapting Planning to Issues

The issues that institutions confront through planning have very different characteristics. Sometimes issues, such as financial health or enrollment, with institution-wide implications are major concerns. At other times, one or more units may face issues that do not have immediate or obvious implications for other areas of the institution. Some issues arise from the concerns of internal constituencies, such as reform of developmental education at Essex, while others come from external sources, such as budget retrenchment at Pennsylvania State. Some issues, regardless of their source, have few advocates while others have strong proponents. Issues can be either strategic (redefining an institution's mission, culture, or programs) or operational (improving services, increasing resources, or resolving some concern). Some issues are intensely political, involving conflicting values resulting from self-interest and ideology, while others primarily concern technical questions.

The institutional experiences described in this volume indicate that, to resolve different types of issues, different mixes of faculty/administrator involvement and different degrees of centralized/decentralized attention are required. As these five institutions knew, or quickly discovered, planning processes must be tailored to reflect the nature of each issue under consideration.

The experiences of the colleges and universities in the NCPGF study were consistent with Dunn's observation that planning must focus on "real" issues to get serious attention. When comprehensive planning processes attempt to deal with topics that are not perceived as significant issues, there is often a lack of serious faculty and administrative commitment. In the following sections, examples from this volume and the NCPGF study illustrate the relationships between various issues and the design of planning processes.

Financial Retrenchment or Budget Reallocation. At Bradford College, severe financial constraints required prompt action. The critical nature of the institution's circumstances led faculty to relinquish certain decision prerogatives to top administrators in order to develop a timely, coherent rescue plan. The faculty apparently believed the college's situation compelled them to support the broadly conceived plans of the new leaders. Significantly, however, Green reports that, with the college's circumstances improving, faculty again will be taking a larger role in initiating and reviewing academic decisions. Similarly, prompt actions to reverse Twente University's fortunes appeared to require considerable administrative initiative. At Essex Community College, reforming the general education curriculum implied potential resource reallocations among academic divisions. Thus the administrative leadership had to negotiate and coordinate these academic decisions while assuring faculty that they would not be harmed by curriculum revisions. Similarly, at Penn State the need to selectively fund unit priorities apparently led to changes in its approach to planning. The "vertical reallocations" undoubtedly required considerable leadership to resolve departmental resistance to losing current or potential resources.

Dooris and Lozier point out that, typically, only about 3 percent of a department's funds are subject to discretionary reallocation. Planning that fails to recognize this reality leads to false expectations and, consequently, disillusionment with the process. They further suggest that because staff equate planning with resource acquisition, planning is not likely to succeed if it is associated with major resource reductions. Similarly, interviews conducted during the NCPGF study revealed that those in institutional subunits viewed planning primarily as a way to obtain more resources and judged processes that did not deliver as wasting their time. The NCPGF survey revealed an interesting dilemma. Most respondents believed planning was most necessary during times of retrenchment but also considered it most difficult to undertake at such times.

These findings and observations do not suggest that planning should be abandoned during periods of adversity but, rather, that a particular kind of planning is required. In these circumstances, the politics of resource reallocation and time constraints may require a more centralized planning process and less open communication of options. Bold leadership is needed to set priorities, make choices, and negotiate with external interests. When the circumstances warrant—and there is sufficient trust and confidence—faculty and staff may be willing, temporarily, to accept centralized leadership. Even if they are distasteful, administrative decisions may be more acceptable when they occur in the context of what is viewed as a legitimate, ongoing process. At such times, planning that is highly participative, open, decentralized, and time-consuming does not appear likely to succeed.

Issues Affecting Several Units. Dooris and Lozier mention the tendency toward compartmentalization that is associated with decentralized decision making. Departments tend to operate somewhat autonomously, and over-decentralization of planning can lead to neglecting issues affecting more than one unit. This tendency poses complications in designing planning processes aimed at resolving issues affecting two or more units. When an issue affects more than one unit, some central direction and active participation by affected areas appears to be required in decision making. At Penn State, the administrative leadership established and supported groups studying issues affecting several academic departments and colleges. At Essex, because decisions on general education requirements affected all academic divisions, campus-wide opportunities for participation were incorporated into the planning process used in determining curriculum revisions. Planning for this issue required administrative coordination and assurances of employment security, together with faculty leadership for developing the program and institution-wide discussions of its merits and potential impact on students and faculty.

Issues Initiated by External Demands. Findings from the NCPGF study suggest that different planning processes are used to address different external demands. Governmental requests are frequently met by centralized and often pro forma institutional processes, typically with limited institutional participation. Responses to marketplace dynamics, however, require a high degree of decentralized decision making and an entrepreneurial culture.

The experiences at Twente and Essex are consistent with these findings. Ringle and Capshaw have described the highly structured and coordinated processes employed to gain state board approval for new programs and facilities. Maassen and van Buchem note the central development and coordination of Twente's response to government planning requirements. Both Essex and Twente, however, emphasizing entrepreneurship and flexibility, found decentralized planning necessary to meet changing external demands for educational programs.

Mission Changes or Revisions. Two of the five institutions undertook significant changes of mission. Bradford redefined its mission and core academic program to make it more attractive to the contemporary student. Twente sought to transform itself from a regional university, dependent on local industry, to a national university with an entrepreneurial orientation. Tufts, while building on its mission, sought to establish major new academic programs that would complement and enhance existing strengths. In all three cases, highly active and visible leaders, with coherent views of their institution's future, played a major role in gaining faculty acceptance and external support for changes these leaders believed to be important. While leaders' visions are critical factors in solving institutional problems, these visions undoubtedly could not have been implemented without cultivating faculty support and dealing sensitively with their concerns and fears. At Bradford, for example, Green describes how actions were taken to restore the faculty's confidence before dealing with major decisions about the character of the college. Had these actions not been taken, the faculty very likely would have unionized, setting up a confrontational situation, and the board of trustees reportedly would have closed the institution.

Basic missions were not in question at Penn State and Essex Community College. Rather, these institutions sought to pursue their missions more effectively. Consequently, their planning efforts focused more on specific issues than broad concerns about institutional character, although perceptions of institutional effectiveness were important.

An institution's mission communicates its general character and the direction in which it intends to proceed. It creates a vision of its role within the higher education system and society. A mission statement sets bounds on appropriate programs and activities and, when changed, implies new emphases and resource reallocations. To be useful, a mission statement should be coherent and represent a reconciliation of conflicting views. Typically, institutional and external constituencies have a stake in the status quo and fear uncertainties associated with change. Therefore mission revisions are controversial and require excellent leadership skills. Consequently, altering a mission requires particularly sensitive attention to where power is located, both inside and outside an institution, and the attitudes of significant constituencies. At Bradford, Tufts, and Twente, new leaders were able to articulate persuasive visions and to garner sufficient trust and acceptance among others to make needed changes.

In contrast to the strategic decisions required when revising an institution's mission, plans guiding resource allocation follow highly structured processes. Participants want to know the rules and be assured that "financial due process" is being observed. Central design and coordination of these processes appeared necessary, but the character of participation was much different. As Ringle and Capshaw have noted, operational planning at Essex involved a great deal of participation but final decisions were made by central officials charged with serving institution-wide interests. These observations suggest that adopting a single process for both strategic and operational planning is not likely to be successful. Perhaps, in their desire to link planning and budgeting, institutions have sought a comprehensive process to serve both purposes rather than multiple processes tailor-made for specific tasks.

Political and Technical Concerns. Many issues involve significant self-interest and value conflicts among participants, while a few primarily involve technical concerns. Green has described how a controversial decision on student internships was delayed and implemented incrementally because of strong initial faculty opposition. She also notes the patience, the willingness to listen, and the negotiating skills required to get agreement on a new salary structure. Dooris and Lozier have noted the broad representation of faculty on study groups that address issues affecting several units' interests. Ringle and Capshaw emphasize the need for processes that generate consensus when revising Essex's general education curriculum.

Planning for Essex's computer services, in contrast, involved a high ratio of technical to political concerns. Consequently, the planning for this issue involved fewer participants, was more centralized, and was coordinated by the data processing department. Similarly, budget planning, though it typically has more extensive political implications than decisions on computer services, has a major technical component that is largely in the domain of administrators. Ringle and Capshaw note that while there was more participation in initial budgetary decision making, final decisions were more tightly controlled by the president and his immediate staff.

Role of Institutional Research

In these five institutions substantive planning functions were performed primarily by those responsible for decision making, not by planning staff. Most of the authors would agree with Ringle and Capshaw that planning is not a separate activity but is embedded in ongoing administrative processes. At both Penn State and Twente, the role of "planning staff" was organizing and supporting planning directed by administrators and faculty responsible for various campus functions. Dunn describes how the role of

Tufts' planning office changed when a new president arrived—from conducting a separate planning process to supporting presidential and others' initiatives. While both Tufts and Essex had staff responsible for supporting planning, Bradford, a small college with limited resources, obtained its support from a variety of institutional sources.

The experiences of these institutions, as well as those in the NCPGF study, confirm the wisdom of using planning staff in a facilitating role, not as The Planners. As Benveniste, in his book *The Politics of Expertise* (1972), points out, planners are apt to encounter serious difficulties if they define their roles in ways that are not politically sensitive to relationships with their patrons and those responsible for implementing plans. Planners can offer advice on the design and maintenance of planning processes, support these processes by serving as a secretariat, provide technical services, coordinate the activities of various groups, point out issues, broker differences, and draft documents for review and approval. But if they attempt to make decisions and take action in others' domains, they are apt to get into trouble.

Conclusion

Planning Process Design. Decisions in higher education institutions are made in many locations, and implementing decisions requires their acceptance by many parties. Each issue addressed by planning involves different mixes of responsibility and interests. Plans that deal with academic matters typically require faculty initiative and acceptance to succeed. Consequently, a culture of faculty entrepreneurship appears to be an important condition for rapid response to academic opportunities and threats. Faculty must be encouraged to take initiatives through appropriate incentives and an organizational climate that encourages risk taking. Time-consuming and costly coordinative and review procedures must be kept to a minimum. Financial authority should be delegated and an emphasis placed on each unit's management responsibilities. A strong faculty role in planning appears most likely to be successful when

- Resources are stable or expanding
- Issues are the province of a single unit
- Constituencies outside the institution do not have a major stake in the issue.

A strong administrative role in decision making appears necessary when

- Resources are reduced or redistributed
- Issues cut across units requiring coordination and brokering
- Issues are unrelated to the primary responsibilities of any existing unit

- Issues involve parties outside the institution
- An institution requires a new or more clearly defined vision of its future.

All planning processes must find a balance between, on the one hand, inattention to collective interests resulting from various constituencies pursuing their self-interests and, on the other, rigid and insensitive centrally imposed definitions of an institution's welfare. Too little attention to institution-wide interests hampers attempts to address emerging threats and opportunities, creates a sense of drift and ennui, and generates external criticism. Overemphasis on institution-wide interests and consistency dampens entrepreneurship, lessens diversity (thus stifling innovation), and creates time-consuming and expensive coordinating and control mechanisms.

Implementing Plans. Most failures of planning efforts did not result from inadequate data, organizational weaknesses, or inappropriate visions, though these charges might be valid in some instances. More frequently difficulties stemmed from using comprehensive processes unsuited to an institution's character or issues or from lack of political support. In addition, past planning efforts frequently raised unrealistic expectations about gaining the resources and support necessary for implementing new ideas and programs, thus generating frustration and disillusionment. Insufficient attention was given to creating conditions for individual and unit entrepreneurship, such as providing financial incentives and reducing the "costs" of getting a proposal acted upon.

Past planning practices often assumed that new ideas came from committees, thereby neglecting the usual, and generally more fruitful, sources of new ideas and initiatives—namely, individual faculty and administrators. Dunn suggests that someone must have a stake in assuring results if a planning process is to achieve results. He observes that constituency-based committees do not always have the commitment and resources to implement a plan. Since groups examining options may be concerned more with issues affecting their own unit, they may underestimate institution-wide benefits and overlook issues that do not have internal proponents. Establishing new programs that lack institutional "champions" (and may even compete for resources with existing units) or seeking mission changes appears to call for administrative initiative but must be accompanied by sufficient faculty trust and confidence to gain their acceptance of proposed courses of action.

The five institutions described in this volume use planning processes that recognize distributions of power and the need for achieving accommodation and compromise. In addition, they have served as learning experiences helping participants to understand the virtues and necessity of proposed changes.

Benefits of Planning. Did these five institutions find strategic planning concepts helpful? The answer appears to be yes—if planning is viewed as an integral part of institutional decision making and not as a separate, formal, comprehensive activity. Their flexible, individually designed approaches to planning helped them achieve many substantive benefits: new missions, new programs, new services, and greater financial strength. They also provided important process benefits. Among them were new institutional cultures or climates, improved communication among units, and increased understanding and consensus.

References

Benveniste, G. *The Politics of Expertise.* Berkeley, Calif.: Glendessary Press, 1972.

Chaffee, E. E. "The Concept of Strategy: From Business to Higher Education." In J. Smart (ed.), *Higher Education: Handbook of Theory and Research.* New York: Agathon Press, 1985.

Cohen, M. D., March, J. G., and Olsen, J. P. "A Garbage Can Model of Organizational Choice." *Administrative Science Quarterly,* 1972, *17* (1), 1–15.

Etzioni, A. "Mixed Scanning: A Third Approach to Decision Making." *Public Administration Review,* 1967, *27,* 387–391.

Lindblom, C. E. "The Science of Muddling Through." *Public Administration Review,* 1959, *19* (2), 79–88.

Lindblom, C. E. *The Policy Making Process.* Englewood Cliffs, N.J.: Prentice-Hall, 1968.

Schmidtlein, F. A. "Decision Process Paradigms in Higher Education." *Educational Researcher,* 1973, *3,* 4–11.

Schmidtlein, F. A., and Milton, T. H. "Campus Planning in the United States: Perspectives from a Nation-Wide Study." *Planning for Higher Education,* 1989, *17* (3), 1–19.

Schmidtlein, F. A., and Milton, T. H. *A Review of Literature on Higher Education Institutional Planning.* College Park: Center for Postsecondary Governance and Finance, University of Maryland, 1990.

Wildavsky, A. "If Planning Is Everything, Maybe It's Nothing." *Policy Sciences,* 1973, *4,* 127–153.

Frank A. Schmidtlein is associate professor of higher education in the Department of Education Policy, Planning, and Administration at the University of Maryland, College Park. He served as director of a nationwide study of institutional planning conducted by the National Center for Postsecondary Governance and Finance and is an associate director of the center.

INDEX

Ordering Information

New Directions for Institutional Research is a series of paperback books that provides planners and administrators in all types of academic institutions with guidelines in such areas as resource coordination, information analysis, program evaluation, and institutional management. Books in the series are published quarterly in Fall, Winter, Spring, and Summer and are available for purchase by subscription as well as by single copy.

Subscriptions for 1990 cost $42.00 for individuals (a savings of 20 percent over single-copy prices) and $56.00 for institutions, agencies, and libraries. Please do not send institutional checks for personal subscriptions. Standing orders are accepted.

Single copies cost $12.95 when payment accompanies order. (California, New Jersey, New York, and Washington, D.C., residents please include appropriate sales tax.) Billed orders will be charged postage and handling.

Discounts for quantity orders are available. Please write to the address below for information.

All orders must include either the name of an individual or an official purchase order number. Please submit your order as follows:
  Subscriptions: specify series and year subscription is to begin
  Single copies: include individual title code (such as IR1)

Mail all orders to:
  Jossey-Bass Inc., Publishers
  350 Sansome Street
  San Francisco, California 94104

OTHER TITLES AVAILABLE IN THE
NEW DIRECTIONS FOR INSTITUTIONAL RESEARCH SERIES
Patrick T. Terenzini Editor-in-Chief
Ellen Earle Chaffee, Associate Editor